TO THE GLORY
OF GOD

To the glory of God

Mormon Essays on Great Issues — Environment-Commitment
Love - Peace -Youth - Man

ENVIRONMENT — COMMITMENT

LOVE — PEACE — YOUTH — MAN

Contributors

Hugh W. Nibley, C. Terry Warner, Reed H. Bradford,
Neal A. Maxwell, David H. Yarn, Jr., Truman G. Madsen,
Chauncey C. Riddle, Robert K. Thomas, Leonard J.
Arrington, Martin B. Hickman, Richard L.
Anderson, Monte S. Nyman

Published by

Deseret Book Company
Salt Lake City, Utah
1972

Library of Congress Catalog Card No. 72-78244
ISBN - 87747-475-3

Copyright 1972 by
Deseret Book Company

Printed in U. S. A.

DEDICATION

To the life and memory of B. West Belnap,
late Dean of the College of
Religious Instruction at
Brigham Young University

FOREWORD
by President Harold B. Lee

I am grateful that the colleagues of B. West Belnap have gathered this group of essays which testify of the things he knew. He knew that we were given this earth as a heritage which we must not pollute, but tend and care for. He knew that without total commitment to the Lord and Savior, life has only fleeting moments of meaning, but with that commitment its plan and meaning become soul-sustaining. West also knew how to love and be loved as the Lord has taught us. He testified in his last days that the greatest thing that had come to him, especially poignantly in his illness, was the love that we bear one another in the love of Christ.

As the colleagues of West Belnap reach out to the youth in the Church with their testimonies, they seek to reflect Jacob's teaching, "To be learned is good if they hearken unto the counsels of God." (2 Nephi 9:29.)

EDITORS' NOTE AND
DEDICATION

When we found out B. West Belnap's two brain-tumor operations had not arrested the malignancy, we sat in wonderment as he spoke to us for his last time as Dean of the College of Religious Instruction at Brigham Young University.

He did not allow himself the luxury of tears. In fact, he seasoned his calm, fluent remarks with his characteristic chuckle, and the timbre of his voice was the evidence of his conviction. It is not the point here to recount his exact words; they were only the husks of his message that reflected the amazements of his recent trauma.

He spoke first of the flood, and the continuing flood, of letters from around the world, from students, from counselees, from people whose lives he had touched. They were not just polite declarations of sympathy, they were specific statements of profound, personal debt for his impact as a teacher.

But, second, there had been pain, redoubled pain, that racked him through his whole being. The day came when he cried out to Brother Harold B. Lee, "Am I to hold on, to keep fighting, or let go?" And he was counseled to "live it out to the last day." "Brethren," he said, "we are taught, we, ourselves, have taught that 'Christ endured afflictions of every kind.' Brethren, if he only endured my kind, the kind I have known in the hospital these past months. . . . Brethren, he loves us much more than we comprehend."

The College of Religious Instruction were honorary pallbearers. We sat together, and during that funeral, much that had distracted us, or loomed to separate us, melted away. It seemed that Elder Harold B. Lee, who was the main speaker that day, was not talking *about* B. West Belnap, but *for* him, when he said:

I sought for something that might be the kind of farewell that I think he would want to say to you. And I'm saying it to you teachers, you his associates, you who are impressing the lives of thousands and thousands of these young people, that if you don't touch them, you religious education teachers, we have lost the souls of men if we teach them nothing but the intellectual things and the physical things. It remains for the teachers in this department to put on the capstone, like West Belnap knew how to put it on, to finish their lives.

This volume represents some of the reverberations of that challenge and charge. These essays, which were written in the spirit that all things should be done with an eye single to the glory of God, share the dedication that was B. West Belnap's life. They are dedicated to a man who was full of truth and responsible feelings for the encounter of what is deepest in man with what is deepest in man's world. Many who knew him will find him between the lines in these essays. Many who did not know him will see more clearly things they thought they knew, but, in fact, did not know well at all. And in these things they will see the One West Belnap came—and left—to serve.

Truman G. Madsen
Charles D. Tate, Jr., Editors

CONTENTS

Brigham Young on the Environment

Hugh W. Nibley

HUGH W. NIBLEY is one of the most gifted scholars in the Church today. His linguistic abilities, his concern with detail, and his brilliant mind combine to make all efforts productive and meaningful. He is a prolific writer and a gifted lecturer.

He graduated summa cum laude from the University of California at Los Angeles, and completed a University Fellow Ph.D. degree at the University of California at Berkeley.

After serving in military intelligence in World War II, he taught at Claremont Colleges in California before joining Brigham Young University, where he spends most of his time in research and writing.

Dr. Nibley was honored as recipient of the David O. McKay Humanities Award. He served as a missionary for the Church in Switzerland and Germany, and concluded his mission in Greece.

He and his wife, the former Phyllis Draper, are the parents of eight children.

BRIGHAM YOUNG
ON THE ENVIRONMENT

Hugh W. Nibley

The Celestial Environment

Brigham Young is one of the few men in history who could claim the privilege of personally occupying, settling, and placing the stamp of his own personality on a large part of the earth's surface. He founded a hundred communities over hundreds of thousands of square miles of the continent, and after over a century they are still in existence, some of them, in those places where the bulldozer and chain saw have not yet completed their devastation, still bearing visibly the marks of his genius. For Brigham was keenly aware of his unique opportunity to lay the foundations of a new civilization and of the awful responsibility that weighed upon anyone who presumed to alter the face of nature and create an environment in which generations yet unborn would be obliged to live.

It does not often fall to the lot of mortal men to set foot, let alone to settle, in a land as fair and undefiled as in the morning of Creation, but that part of the world into which Brigham Young finally led the Mormons was such a land. It was their privilege to lay the foundations of Zion in a region of the globe that man had not visibly altered or defiled, amid scenes of rare and startling beauty in a fresh and unspoiled world. "You are here commencing anew," he told the people. "The soil, the air, the water are all pure and healthy. Do not suffer them to become polluted with wickedness. Strive to preserve the elements from being contaminated by the filthy wicked conduct and sayings of those who pervert the intelligence God has bestowed upon the hu-

man family." (8:79:60.)[1] For Brigham, moral and physical
cleanliness and pollution are no more to be separated than
mind and body: "Keep your valley pure, keep our towns as
pure as you possibly can, keep your hearts pure, and labor
what you can consistently, but not so as to injure yourselves.
Be faithful in your religion. Be full of love and kindness to-
wards each other." (8:80:60.) There is nothing mysterious
or abstruse in this identifying of the defilement of man with
the defilement of nature. A Latter-day Saint astronomer has
recently written, "Pollution and environmental deterioration
are primarily moral and spiritual problems, rather than problems of technology."[2]

At a time when "free as air" signified that a thing
was of negligible worth, Brigham Young was insisting that
the greatest physical asset the Saints possessed and one they
should treasure most highly was pure air. "What constitutes
health, wealth, joy and peace? In the first place, good pure
air is the greatest sustainer of animal life." (MS 22:748:60.)[3]
"The Lord blesses the land, the air and the water where the
Saints are permitted to live." (10:222:63.) "We have the
sweet mountain air, and a healthy country. . . . What kind
of air did you breathe, who lived in eleven, twelve, and
fourteen story houses in your native country?" (1:78:53.)
"Speaking of the elements and the creation of God, in their
nature they are pure as the heavens." (8:341:61.) But since
the earth is a place of testing, "every faculty bestowed upon
man is subject to contamination—subject to be diverted from
the purpose the Creator designed it to fill" (6:94:57); and
it is so with all things in this world. Accordingly, "the
strength, power, beauty, and glory that once adorned the
form and constitution of man have vanished away before the
blighting influences of inordinate appetite and love of this
world." (12:118:67.) The pressure is always on: "Our ene-

[1]Unless otherwise indicated, references given hereafter are from the
Journal of Discourses. The first number indicates the volume, the second the
page, and the third the year of excerpt.
[2]A. B. Morrison in *New Era* 1:69 (1971).
[3]MS indicates the *Millennial Star,* with volume, page, and year following.

mies . . . would like to see society in Utah polluted, and their civilization introduced; but it would be a wo[e]ful day for the Israel of God, if such efforts were to be successful." (*MS* 27:205f:65.)

Why should the enemy seek to pollute? There was an early Christian teaching, reported by Eusebius, that the evil spirits, being forever deprived of physical bodies, constantly go about in the world jealously seeking to defile and corrupt such bodies, glorying in foulness and putrefaction as they "move about in thick, polluted air," and make charnel houses and garbage dumps their favorite haunts,[4] until the earth cries out: "Wo, wo is me, the mother of men. . . . When shall I rest, and be cleansed from the filthiness which is gone forth out of me?" (Moses 7:48.) Once in reply to that cry a vast outpouring of waters purged the earth, quite literally, of its filthiness.

It was an awesome task that the Mormons were undertaking in laying the foundations of Zion; it meant preparing a fit habitation for the Saints, an environment and an economy stable enough to last a thousand years, a setting worthy to receive and entertain the visits of heavenly beings, a place that in time the Lord himself would be pleased to call his permanent home! Yet Brigham did not hesitate for a moment to launch into the work with perfect confidence and astounding elan—before the Saints had been in the valley a single day, ditches, fields, and streets had been laid out and the water was running into garden patches.

Observers of the work that followed often remarked with awe that Brother Brigham seemed to know exactly what he was doing all the time. He did know, for this master builder and craftsman had been given the most perfect of models to work with, nothing less than the heavenly order as revealed to the Prophet Joseph. "We are trying to be the image of those who live in heaven; we are trying to pattern after them, to look like them, to walk and talk like them, to deal

---

[4]Eusebius, *Praeparatio Evangelica* 5:2 (in Migne, *Patrol. Graec.* 21:313).

like them, and build up the kingdom of heaven as they have
done." (9:170:62.) Yes, but what is heaven really like? We
know that too, according to Joseph F. Smith, a disciple of
Brigham; for that we have only to look about us: "Heaven
was the prototype of this beautiful creation when it came
from the hand of the Creator and was pronounced 'good.' "
(23:175:82.)

When Dr. Morrison, the astronomer, compares this earth
to "an exquisitely equipped spaceship" on which every human want has been anticipated and provided for,[5] he might
be paraphrasing the scriptures that tell us that this earth has
been prepared with "all things . . . made for the benefit and
the use of man, both to please the eye and to gladden the
heart; yea, for food and for raiment, for taste and for smell,
to strengthen the body and to enliven the soul." (D&C 59:
18-19.) Or as Brigham Young puts it, "All the creations are
His work, and they are for His glory and for the benefit of
the children of men; and all things are put into the possession
of man for his comfort, improvement and consolation, and
for his health, wealth, beauty and excellency." (13:151:69.)

His words of a hundred years ago strongly suggest the
image of the spaceship today: "The earth is very good in and
of itself, and has abided a celestial law; consequently, we
should not despise it, nor desire to leave it, but rather desire
and strive to obey the same law that the earth abides."
(2:302-3:55.) "Our business is not merely to prepare to go
to another planet. This is our home." (8:297:60.) "We are
for the kingdom of God, and are not going to the moon, nor
to any other planet pertaining to this solar system. . . . This
earth is the home he has prepared for us, and we are to prepare ourselves and our habitations for the celestial glory in
store for the faithful." (8:293-94:60.)

But if the work has already been done, all the physical
arrangement completed and the vessel a model of perfection
at the time we set foot on the deck, what remains for us to

---

[5]Morrison, p. 65; Joseph Fielding Smith, *Teachings of the Prophet Joseph
Smith* (Salt Lake City: Deseret Book Co., 1970), p. 248.

do on it and with it? That is for us to find out first of all, according to Brigham, examining the structure with care, studying its nature and possibilities meticulously, considering well before we lay about us with gun, fire, and plow. "It is one of the most happifying subjects that can be named, for a person, or people, to have the privilege of gaining wisdom enough while in their mortal tabernacle . . . and understand the design of the Great Maker of this beautiful creation." (1:111:53.) "Field and mountains, trees and flowers, and all that fly, swim, or move upon the ground are lessons for study in the great school of our Heavenly Father, in what is before us in good books and in the greater laboratory of nature." (9:320:62.)

If the earth still retained its paradisiacal glory, we would be justified in asking, "What do we do now?" But that glory has departed, and the first step in the rebuilding of Zion is to help bring it back. "Who placed the dark stain of sin upon this fair creation? Man. Who but man shall remove the foul blot, and restore all things to their primeval purity and innocence? [That is a large order, an impossible assignment, and Brigham admits it.] But can he do this independent of heavenly aid? He cannot. To aid him in this work heavenly grace is here." (10:301:64.) Fortunately it is God's work, in which he allows us to participate. "The greatest acts of the mighty men," said Joseph Smith, have been disastrous. "Before them the earth was a paradise, and behind them a desolate wilderness. . . . The designs of God, on the other hand" are that "the earth shall yield its increase, resume its paradisean glory, and become as the garden of the Lord."[6] It is a clear-cut and fundamental doctrine: "We believe . . . that Christ will reign personally upon the earth; and, that the earth will be renewed and receive its paradisiacal glory." (Tenth Article of Faith.) That, however, according to the same Article of Faith, will be the last step of five in the rehabilitation of the earth, and according to Brigham Young, it was to be a long hard pull: "Not many generations will pass away before the days of man will again

return. But it will take generations to entirely eradicate the
influences of deleterious substances. This must be done before
we can attain our paradaical [sic] state." (8:64:60.)

But what about eternal progression? Is the best we can
hope for a reversion to the primordial state of the earth? Man
is not an intangible Ariel; he walks with solid tread and leaves
his mark on everything he touches. God is quite aware of
that—he planned it that way: "Behold, the Lord hath created the earth that it should be inhabited; and he hath created
his children that they should possess it." (1 Ne. 17:36.)

No one appreciated this better than the supremely solid
and practical Brigham Young. Along with a deep-seated
reverence for God's establishment, he had a New England
Yankee's passion for "improvement." "What is this work?"
he asks. "The improvement of the condition of the human
family. This work must continue until the people who live on
this earth are prepared to receive our coming Lord." (19:46:
77.) Day by day the prophet never tired in giving full and
explicit instructions on just what the people should do to
improve:

> There is a great work for the Saints to do. Progress, and improve
> upon, and make beautiful everything around you. Cultivate the earth and
> cultivate your minds. Build cities, adorn your habitations, make gardens,
> orchards, and vineyards, and render the earth so pleasant that when you
> look upon your labours you may do so with pleasure, and that angels
> may delight to come and visit your beautiful locations." (8:83:60.)

For Brigham, improvement meant "to build in strength
and stability, to beautify, to adorn, to embellish, to delight,
and to cast fragrance over the House of the Lord; with
sweet instruments of music and melody." (MS 10:86:48.)

Specifically, the one way man can leave his mark on the
face of nature without damage is to plant, and President
Young ceaselessly counseled his people to do as Adam was
commanded to do in Eden—when he dressed and tended the
garden: Our work is "to beautify the face of the earth, until
it shall become like the Garden of Eden." (1:345:53.) "The

very object of our existence here is to handle the temporal elements of this world and subdue the earth, multiplying those organisms of plants and animals God has designed shall dwell upon it." (9:168:62.)

Where men cannot foresee the distant effects of their actions on the environment because of the vastly complicated interrelationships of the balance of nature, what rule of action shall they follow? Brigham was never in doubt: the one sure guide for him was the feeling for beauty; he knew with Plato that the good, the true, and the beautiful are the same; that what looks and feels and sounds and tastes good is to that degree sound, useful, and trustworthy: "You watch your own feelings when you hear delightful sounds . . . or when you see anything beautiful. Are those feelings productive of misery? No, they produce happiness, peace, and joy." (12:314:68.) We can trust such feelings, for "every flower, shrub, and tree to beautify, and to gratify the taste and smell, and every sensation that gives man joy and felicity are for the Saints who receive them from the Most High." (9:244:62.) "Who gave the lower animals a love for those sweet sounds, which with magic power fill the air with harmony, and cheer and comfort the hearts of men, and so wonderfully affect the brute creation? It was the Lord, our Heavenly Father, who gave the capacity to enjoy these sounds, and which *we* ought to do in His name, and to His glory." (1:48:52.)

To the objection that some people have atrocious taste, Brigham has the answer. If taste, like mind and muscle, is a thing we are born with, it is no less a thing that we are under sacred obligation to cultivate and train properly. We enjoy because we have sensibility. Promote this sensibility, seek to get more and more knowledge, more wisdom, and more understanding. . . . This will give us greater sensibility, and we shall know how to enjoy, and how to endure. I say, if you want to enjoy exquisitely, become a Latter-day Saint and then live the doctrine of Jesus Christ." (18:246-47:74.)

Taste can be cultivated and so must be: "Let us . . . show
to the world that we have talent and taste, and prove to the
heavens that our minds are set on beauty and true excellence,
so that we can become worthy to enjoy the society of angels."
(11:305:67.)

It is through "greater sensibility" that we both enjoy
and endure, for the appreciation of beauty is nothing less
than the key to survival. Nature has so provided that we
actually enjoy most doing and sensing the very things most
conducive to our survival; we delight in performing the most
vital functions of life, and so simply by enjoying ourselves,
we build up more formidable defenses against the powers
of destruction than any accumulation of scientific data or
learned admonition could provide. We eat long before we
are in danger of dying of hunger and drink long before
reaching a critical stage of dehydration, simply because we
enjoy eating and drinking. If we ate, drank, breathed, and
slept only when persuaded by irrefutable scientific demonstration that if we did not do those things we would die, we
would not be long for this world. So it is in all things, and
creatures as weak and vulnerable as man must cultivate a
salutary sense of what is lovely and desirable and what is
wrong and threatening, a feeling that hits them long before
they can tell just why a thing is to be welcomed or dreaded.

"When the Spirit of revelation from God inspires a man,
his mind is opened to behold the beauty, order, and glory of
the creation of this earth." How does such a one react when
"a man says, 'I am going to make iron, and I will have the
credit of making the first iron in the Territory' "? He can
only feel that "the beauty and glory of this kind of proceeding is the blackest of darkness, and its comeliness as de-
formity." (9:256-57:62.) Why so? Without being able to
tell exactly why, we take immediate offense at such statements, made by men in high positions, as "I do not believe in
conservation for conservation's sake," or "I do not believe in
clean water for the sake of clean water." But we soon learn

that our shocked first reaction is a healthy one; when the forest is reduced to the now proverbial one redwood, it is too late. What prevents such a catastrophe is not the logic of survival but the feelings of wrongness. "Are you not dissatisfied," asks Brigham Young, "and is there not bitterness in your feelings, the moment you find a kanyon put in the possession of an individual, and power given unto him to control the timber, wood, rock, grass, and, in short, all its facilities? Does there not something start up in your breast, that causes you to feel very uncomfortable?" (1:210:52.) Brigham does not apologize for his feelings; the Puritan ethic, which he knew and despised so well, would salve its conscience by putting virtue on the side of the cash box and making a great show of abstemiousness not from greed but from the delights that God means us to have: "But the greater portion of the sectarian world consider it sacrilege to give way to any such pleasure as even to listen to sweet music, much more to dance to its delightful strains." (1:48: 52.) The voice of revelation has told the Saints, however, where to put their priorities: "And out of the ground made I, the Lord God, to grow every tree, naturally, that is pleasant to the sight of man; and man could behold it." (Moses 3:9.) Trees were made in the first instance to be looked at and enjoyed; we are aware of that before research and experience show our intuition to be quite sound—but the feeling for beauty must come first if we are to survive.

Use All Gently

It behooves us as fortunate visitors in the King's palace to behave circumspectly, to look and admire, damage nothing, take nothing with us, and leave everything as nearly as possible as we found it. Restraint is the watchword in dealing with God's earth: The products of the earth are "to please the eye [that always comes first!] and to gladden the heart; yea, for food and for raiment, for taste and for smell . . . to be used with judgment, not to excess neither by extortion."

(D&C 59:18-20.) We may neither waste nor exploit what we find around us; Webster defines *extortion* as "undue exaction; specifically, an oppression by color of right." We have a right to take what we need, but when we would extend that right to justify taking things we do not need, that is extortion, and is expressly forbidden: "It is our privilege and our duty," says Brigham Young, "to search all things upon the face of the earth, and lean what there is for man to enjoy, what God has ordained for the benefit and happiness of mankind, and then make use of it without sinning against him." (9:243:62.) Sinning against him? "It is not our privilege to waste the Lord's substance." (11:126:65.)

For "whatever you have, it is the Lord's. You own nothing, I own nothing. . . . The Lord has placed what I have in my hands, to see what I will do with it. . . . I have neither wife nor child, no wives and children; they are only committed to me, to see how I will treat them. If I am faithful, the time will come when they will be given to me." (10:298:64.) The same applies to the world of nature, which we also hold in trust: "Not one particle of all that comprises this vast creation of God is our own. Everything we have has been bestowed upon us for our action, to see what we would do with it—whether we would use it for eternal life and exaltation, or for eternal death and degradation." (8:67:60.) We are being tested to demonstrate to the heavens, to ourselves, and to our fellows just how we would treat the things of a glorious and beautiful world if they were given to us as our very own.

Those who insist on "clinging to the earth" as if they owned it have forever disqualified themselves from receiving hereafter the mandate: "There is a vast eternity stretched out before you; now organize as you will." (8:341:61.) We are placed in the position of a lover who is engaged to be married; if he cannot wait until he is properly wed, or if he displays an arrogant and brutal nature toward his promised bride, then the wedding had best be called off—he is not worthy of the prize.

"We should love the earth," says Brigham. "We should love the works which God has made. This is correct; but we should love them in the Lord." (11:112:65.) We should look forward to a time when this earth "will be given to the Saints, when they and it are sanctified and glorified, and brought back into the presence of the Father and the Son." (15:127: 72.) But that time is not yet; the question is, Can we wait? *"Why do men set their hearts upon them in their present organized state?* Why not lay a sure foundation to control them hereafter?" (1:272:53.)

We may enjoy these things in anticipation, but in doing so we must display the spirit that shows we can be trusted: "It is the privilege of the Saints to enjoy every good thing, for the earth and its fulness belong to the Lord, and he has promised all to his faithful Saints; but it must be enjoyed without [the] spirit of covetousness and selfishness." (8:82:60.) That is where all but a few fail the test: "The earth is organized for a glorious resurrection, and life and death are set before the people, true riches and false riches; and the whole world are gone after the false riches." (1:274:53.)

To honor God's creation is a high moral principle with Brigham Young. First, because it is God's wonderful work and bears his mark upon it, and man, try as he will, is in no position to improve on it. "Man's machinery makes things alike; God's machinery gives to things which appear alike a pleasing difference. . . . Endless variety is stamped upon the works of God's hand. There are no two productions of nature, whether animal, vegetable, or mineral, that are exactly alike [N.B. when you've seen one, you have *not* seen them all!], and all are crowned with a degree of polish and perfection that cannot be obtained by ignorant man in his most exquisite mechanical productions." (9:369-70:62.)

Frankly, Brigham was not much impressed by "progress": "The civilized nations know how to make machinery, put up telegraph wires, &c., &c.; and in nearly all branches they are trying to cheat each other, . . . they have been cheat-

ing themselves for the golden god—the Mammon of this
world." (*MS* 22:741:60.) They think it wonderful to "dwell
amid the whirl of mental and physical energies, constantly
taxed to their utmost tension in the selfish, unsatisfying and
frenzied quest of worldly emolument, fame, power, and
maddening draughts from the syren cup of pleasure." (*MS*
20:218:57.) Having "obtained the promise that he should be
father of lives, in comparison with this, what did Abraham
care about machinery, railroads, and other great mechanical
productions?" (8:63:60.)

In the second place, we should use extreme restraint,
because it is immoral and foolish to destroy what we cannot
replace. As Joseph F. Smith, Brigham Young's disciple, was
wont to quote: "Take not away the life you cannot give,
For all things have an equal right to live."[6] "Did you ever
organize a tree, gold, silver, or any other kind of metal, or
any other natural production? No, you have not yet attained
to that power, and it will be ages before you do. Who owns
all the elements with which we are commanded and permitted
to operate? The Lord, and we are stewards over them." (4:
29:56.) By their own manipulations and sophistries, men get
legal authority to destroy what they will of nature, but
Brigham Young believed that "a man has no right to property, which, according to the laws of the land, legally belongs to him, if he does not want to use it . . . to do good
to himself and his fellow-man." (1:252:53.)

Not only have we no right to rifle the treasury that God
has laid up for coming generations on the earth, but we can
never justify such plunder on the plea of necessity. "If we
have our hundreds or thousands we may foster the idea that
we have nothing more than we need; but such a notion is
entirely erroneous, for our real wants are very limited. What
do we absolutely need? I possess everything on the face of the
earth that I need, as I appear before you on this stand. . . . I
have everything that a man needs or can enjoy if he owned

----

[6]*Gospel Doctrine* (Salt Lake City: Deseret Book Company) 1:371-72
(Melchizedek Priesthood manual, 1970-71).

the whole world. If I were the king of the earth I could enjoy no more." (*MS* 32:818-19:70.) "When you have that you wish to eat and sufficient clothing to make you comfortable, you have all that you need; I have all that I need." (13:302: 70.) "I do not desire to keep a particle of my property, except enough to protect me from a state of nudity." (4:55: 56.)

Paradoxically, we are learning to live *without* things so that we can learn to live *with* things. God wants us to "handle the gold and silver of the whole earth without having a desire for it, only as a means with which to gather Israel, redeem Zion, subdue and beautify the earth, and bring all things in readiness to live with God in heaven." (3:160:55.) As long as we go on accumulating stuff in this life, we are playing the devil's game, for "there is no such thing as a man being truly rich until he has power over death, hell, the grave, and him that hath the power of death, which is the devil." (1:271:53.) We will have a right to do as we please with our own only "when we can speak to the earth—to the native elements in boundless space, and say to them—'Be ye organized, and planted here, or there, and stay until I command you hence.' " (1:269:53.)

Sin Is Waste

Brigham Young had a Yankee passion also for thrift, but it rested on a generous respect for the worth of things and not on a niggardly desire to possess them. When he says, "I do not know that, during thirty years past, I have worn a coat, hat, or garment of any kind, or owned a horse, carriage, &c., but what I asked the Lord whether I deserved it or not —Shall I use this? Is it mine to use, or not?" (8:343:61), he is expressing the highest degree of human concern and responsibility. "If I have horses, oxen, and possessions, they are the Lord's and not mine; and all I ask is for him to tell me what to do with them." (6:46:57.) "Without the Spirit of the Lord Jesus Christ, we cannot enjoy the good things of

life." (8:82:60.) But with it we need never feel guilty: "It
is the privilege of the Saints to enjoy every good thing, for
the earth and its fulness belong to the Lord." (8:82:60.) It
is a magnanimous thrift that never hesitates to take and
spend whatever is needed but under no circumstances will
touch a molecule more. We may take all we need, because it
is the Lord's but wo to him who dares to take more—for it
is the Lord's! This is the exact reverse of the world's economy. Who would expect our most competent businessman to
proclaim as his slogan, "Never count the cost"? "If I am
going to build a temple, I am not going to sit down and
count the cost. I care not what it will cost. I have built
a great many houses, and never counted the cost before I
built them. I never wanted to know anything about it."
(8:355:61.) "I have built what I have built without asking
how much they cost, or where I was to get the money to
do it." (17:158:74.) "When the Saints are required to
embark in any public enterprise, the word should not be . . .
'What will it cost, and will it pay, etc.?' but, 'It is a work
for the public good, and we can do it.' " (10:362:64.) Strange
as such a policy may seem, it is but the honest expression of
the belief that God really does own everything and that he
really will provide. "When we learn this lesson, where will be
my interest and my effort?" Certainly not in personal acquisition: "Every man and woman has got to feel that not one
farthing of anything in their possession is rightfully theirs."
(4:29:56.)

All waste on this earth becomes garbage—*waste* is in
fact the proper English word for garbage. To throw anything on the trash heap is to cast it aside in contempt; what
do we know about its true worth? Who are we to despise
what we do not understand? *"Never let anything go to waste.
Be prudent, save everything."* (1:250:53.) Even sewage has
its uses: "Everything, also, which will fertilize our gar-
dens and our fields should be sedulously saved and wisely
husbanded, that nothing may be lost which contains the elements of food and raiment for man and sustenance for beast."

(11:130:65.) Brigham was aware of one of the basic facts of economy, that man, whatever he may say, does not create or produce—he merely takes:

> Man cannot control the heavens; he cannot control the earth, nor the elements; he can fertilize and prepare the ground for the reception of seed; he can plant, water, till, and reap . . . but until his mind is opened by the Spirit of God, he cannot see that it is by a superior power that corn, wheat, and every kind of vegetation spring into life, and ripen for the sustenance of man and beast. (3:119:55.)

Moreover, "we cannot own anything, in the strict sense of the word, until we have the power to bring into existence and hold in existence, independent of all other powers." (8:118:60.)

Since man cannot create, he must face up to the number one fact of ecology, which Brigham Young enunciated long before even the scientific community began to take it seriously: "There is only so much property in the world. There are the elements that belong to this globe, and no more. We do not go to the moon to borrow; neither send to the sun or any of the planets; all our commercial transactions must be confined to this little earth, and its wealth cannot be increased or diminished." To this he adds the observation —over one hundred years ago—that the resources of the earth are being placed out of our reach by an irreversible process of buying short-term prosperity on promissory notes that science will never be able to make good: "And though the improvements in the arts of life which have taken place within the memory of many now living are very wonderful, there is no question that extravagance has more than kept pace with them." (13:304:70.) The dangerous policy of converting all into cash as quickly as possible is another expression of that lack of faith that will invest nothing in a hereafter: "It is all good, the air, the water, the gold and silver; the wheat, the fine flour, and the cattle upon a thousand hills are all good. . . . But the moment that men seek to build up themselves . . . and seek to hoard up riches it proves that their hearts are weaned from their God; *and their riches will perish in their fingers, and they with them."* (1:272:53; italics added.) It is natural for anyone to grab what he can get when he can get it, but "who will commit to that man or woman the great things of the kingdom of God that are to be attained on this earth" when the time comes? (8:295:60.)

Brigham in Action

On March 27, 1846, as the Saints were about to go forth on the first leg of their long journey west, we find President Young charging "the Captains in particular to instruct their respective divisions, to be very careful about setting the Prairie or woods on fire . . . to prohibit all discharge of fire arms in the camp and to keep their guns and pistols out of sight."[7] A month later, as the first company moved out, he reported in his journal: "Traveled 19 miles. The prairie appeared black being covered with immense herds of buffalo. May 7th. I preached in camp and advised the brethren not to kill any more buffalo or other game until the meat was needed."[8] To appreciate the farsightedness of the man, let us recall that twenty years after he gave this warning against fires, the youthful Mark Twain sat in a canoe on Lake Tahoe and watched with delight as the flames spread from his *own* campfire to set all the woods ablaze in a holocaust that destroyed everything "as far as the eye could reach the lofty mountain fronts."[9] All he could think of was the splendor of the spectacle, for in his eyes the forests of the West were inexhaustible and men could do as they pleased with them.

As to the buffalo, on a single day in the year 1884 Buffalo Bill killed 285 of them and left their carcasses rotting on the plains. In the following two years the last of the great herds disappeared, but William Cody instead of going to jail

---

[7]*Brigham Young History*, Manuscript in Church Historian's Office, under March 17, 1846.
[8]Ibid., p. 88.
[9]Mark Twain (S. L. Clemens), *Roughing It*, chap. 23.

became a national hero.[10] So far were the Americans, forty years after Brigham Young's admonition, from feeling the necessity of exercising the restraint which he felt so urgent in our contacts with nature.

All who attended, at President Young's invitation, the great 24th of July celebrations at Brighton "were requested to show their tickets at the gate" to the canyon road. The tickets were free, and on them was printed: "All Persons are forbidden to make or kindle fires at any place in the kanyon, except on the camp ground." (MS 18:673ff:56.) A hundred years later people in Utah still resent limitations on camp-fires as an infringement on their God-given freedom. The prophet ended his 24th of July speech with a ritual admoni-tion "to see that the fires are well put out" (ibid., p. 679). The event at Brighton was magnificent enough to get cov-erage in the eminent *New York Herald,* and the reporter who described the doings in the year 1860 tells how at dusk of the last day, after all the wagons had gone home and the dust had settled on the canyon road, he beheld a singular spec-tacle: "By 9 o'clock the last team had left the camp-ground"; but one man remained behind "to see that all the fires were extinguished." And who should that man be but Brigham Young: " 'The Prophet' left the last, satisfied that all was right, and that his disciples had enjoyed themselves to their hearts' content; and thus ended the great celebration of 1860." (MS 22:702:60)

Reverence for Everything

What guided and prescribed the teachings and acts of this great man in all his earthly dealings seems to be before all else his constant awareness of being in the presence of the Divine. To the picnicker at Brighton, he said, "Here are the stupendous works of the God of Nature, though all do not appreciate His wisdom as manifested in his works. . . .

---

[10]On the passing of the buffalo, see the final chapters of J. W. Schultz, *My Life Among the Indians* (Boston, 1941), especially chap. 34.

I could sit here for a month and reflect on the mercies of God." (MS 18:675:56.) Everything around him reminds him of what is holy:

In gazing upon the intelligence reflected in the countenances of my fellow-beings, I gaze upon the image of Him whom I worship—the God I serve. I see His image and a certain amount of His intelligence there. I feel it within myself. My nature shrinks at the divinity we see in others. (13:171:70.)

It is seldom that I rise before a congregation without feeling a child-like timidity; if I live to the age of Methusaleh I do not know that I shall outgrow it. There are reasons for this which I understand . . . this mortality shrinks before that portion of divinity which we inherit from our Father. This is the cause of my timidity. (13:139:69.)

Where is the man who can rise to address children without feeling this same modesty? (13:170:70.)

This same reverence, which the Greeks called *aidos*, for Brigham Young extends to all things; for if life is holy, for him "there is not a particle of element which is not filled with life, and all space is filled with element." (3:277:56.) "Well, how many lives are there in this grain of corn? They are innumerable, and this same infinity is manifest through all the creations of God." (15:138:72.) "There is life in all matter, throughout the vast extent of all the eternities; it is in the rock, the sand, the dust, the water, the air." (3:277: 56.)

This vitalism, supported by interesting and ingenious physical speculations that we cannot go into here, was something that Brigham Young felt very strongly. He laid special emphasis on the importance of human esteem for the animal world, for one of the peculiar doctrines of the Latter-day Saints is that animals are living souls destined to partici-pate in the resurrection as they did in the preexistence. "Learn to control yourselves and that which is immediately around you, and always keep in view that the animal, vege-table, and mineral kingdoms—the earth and its fulness—will all, except the children of men, abide their creation—the law

by which they were made, and will receive their exaltation."
8:191:60.) "Every tree . . . that is pleasant also to the sight
of man . . . became also a living soul. For it was spiritual in
the day that I created it; for it remaineth in the sphere in
which I, God, created it. . . . Every beast of the field . . . they
were also living souls." (Moses 3:9.) The four beasts of Revelation are symbolic animals, but they denote that very real
"happiness of man, and of beasts, and of creeping things, and
of the fowls of the air" in "the paradise of God . . . that
which is spiritual being in the likeness of that which is temporal; and that which is temporal in the likeness of that
which is spiritual. The spirit of man in the likeness of his
person, and also the spirit of beast, and every other creature
which God has created." (D&C 77:2.)

Granted there are different levels and degrees that exist
within as well as between species, still it is the privilege of
every form of life to multiply in its sphere and element and
have joy therein. Adam's dominion was a charge to see to it
that all went well with God's creatures; it was not a license
to exterminate them:

> Every living creature that moveth . . . and every winged fowl after
> its kind . . . all things which I created were good, and I God blessed
> them, saying: Be fruitful, and multiply, and fill the waters in the sea;
> and let the fowl multiply in the air, and everything that creepeth upon
> the earth . . . I God saw that all these things were good. (Moses 2:21.)

There is a forgotten teaching of the early Jews and
Christians that the dominion that God gave to Adam in
Eden over His other creatures was nothing less than the holy
priesthood, the power to act in God's stead. In making His
covenant with Abraham, God is represented as saying to him,
"As I put Adam and then Noah in charge of all my creatures,
so now I put you in charge, and order you to give them my
blessing."[11] To Adam He said, "From now on it is all given
over into your hand, and the creatures will fear you as they

---

[11]Midrash Ps. I, 5; other Midrash passages in M.J. bin Gorion, *Die Sagen
der Juden* (Frankfurt, 1914), 2:17f, 424.

fear me."[12] Accordingly, Adam enjoys God's authority only insofar as he exercises it as God himself would, with perfect love and understanding.

"Even the fierce beasts of prey," says the Zohar, "fear man as long as he keeps his covenant, his kingly dignity, and his eye fixed upon God in whose image he is."[13] Adam's calling, says an equally venerable source, was to take care of the animals, not to dispose of them as his property. The spirits of all beasts have their proper paradise, and at the judgment man will have to give an exact accounting of how he has treated them.[14] "Man by his sovranty [sic] over nature resembles God," says an early Christian writing, "but he enjoys that authority only as long as he behaves in a godlike manner."[15] Only in a noble, generous, and forbearing spirit can the powers of the priesthood be exercised (D&C 121:36-46), and to that spirit in us all creatures have a right to appeal.

"It is not only wicked to destroy them," said Joseph F. Smith, speaking of "our innocent little birds . . . it is abominable, in my opinion. I think that this principle should extend, not only to the bird life, but to the life of all animals. . . . I have known men—and they still exist among us—who enjoy what is, to them, the 'sport' of hunting birds . . . (the birds having had a season of protection and not apprehending danger)—that makes it worse than wicked—it is base, contemptible, ignoble: It is wrong, and I have been surprised at the prominent men whom I have seen whose very souls seem to be athirst for the shedding of animal blood. They go off hunting deer, antelope, elk, anything they can find, and what for? 'Just for the fun of it.' "[16]

When the famous missionary Mildred Cable asked the inhabitants of a remote oasis in the Gobi Desert why they did

---

[12]bin Gorion, 1:82f.
[13]Zohar 1:191f.
[14]This is explained in the *Book of the Secrets of Enoch* (Slavonic text, II Enoch), chap. 15.
[15]V. Aptowitzer in *Revue des Etudes Juives* 75 (1922), pp. 4-6, citing St. Ephraim and other early Christian and Jewish teachers on the subject.
[16]Joseph F. Smith, *Gospel Doctrine*, 1:71-72.

not still their hunger by eating the doves that visited the place in large numbers, they replied that "to trap and eat a pigeon would be contrary to all right feeling, and the oasis dwellers' standard of ethics would not admit that a gentle, harmless, self-constituted guest like a wild bird could be deceived, slain, and devoured. 'The Princely Man,' he would say, 'is not a betrayer of trust.' "[17] God will justify the taking of animal life to sustain man's want, but He reserves a special blessing for those who place their own nobility before their necessity.

This is strikingly illustrated in Brigham Young's declarations regarding the meanest, most repulsive and destructive of creatures—the crickets of the plague. "Last season when the grasshoppers came on my crops, I said, 'Nibble away, I may as well feed you as to have my neighbors do it; I have sown plenty, and you have not raised any yourselves.' And when the harvest came you would not have known that there had been a grasshopper there." The moral of this, he says, is "Pay attention to what the Lord requires of you and let the balance go." (3:159:55.) Years later it came again: "According to present appearances, next year [1868] we may expect grasshoppers to eat up nearly all our crops. But if we have provisions enough to last us another year, we can say to the grasshoppers—these creatures of God—you are welcome. I have never had a feeling to drive them from one plant in my garden; but I look upon them as the armies of the Lord." (12:121:67.)

The Day of the Destroyer

Because of the Fall, man has become the enemy of his own environment, at odds with the whole creation, allergic to all manner of things good in themselves that afflict and torment him: "The animal, vegetable, and mineral kingdoms abide the law of their Creator; the whole earth and all things pertaining to it, except man, abide the law of their creation."

---

[17]M Cable and F. French, *The Gobi Desert* (New York: Macmillan, 1944), p. 114.

(9:246:62.) Conflict is inevitable, with man stubbornly re-
fusing to "become subject to the most sensible and self-
exalting principles," determined to subdue the earth in
his way. "We see all the world trying to lord it over God's
heritage; it is in this spirit that the evil principle and power
is trying to overcome and rule over the divine principle
planted there. This constantly leads the children of men
astray." (9:107:60.) So there is a fundamental conflict here,
and it goes back to the beginning. It is said that Satan ap-
proached Adam with certain propositions that he later presented to Cain, Noah, Abraham, and Job,[18] in which he set
forth his plan for running things: (1) He claimed all
of God's earth, "most glorious and beautiful" from end to
end for his own; (2) then he put up everything in it for sale
to anyone who had the money; (3) and finally he revealed the
source of power and dominion under his system: it all rested
on possession of the treasures of the earth, with which one
can buy any military and political power necessary to rule,
or rather misrule, among the children of men. John Taylor,
Brigham Young's great successor, told the story in simple
verse:

> This world was once a garden place,
> With all its glories common,
> And men did live a holy race
> And worship Jesus face to face,
> In Adam-ondi-Ahman.

That was long ago, when "Enoch walked with God above the
power of Mammon,"[19] but it was this power of mammon
that changed the whole picture. Two fatal flaws stand between us and that time foreseen by Brother Taylor, "when

---

[18]Satan's confrontation with Adam (bin Gorion, op. cit., 1:255) and his
shrewd business propositions were also repeated in the case of Noah (Midrash
Rabbah Noah 36:3 end; bin Gorion 1:226). The Testament of Job follows the
story of Abraham; particularly enlightening is the conversation between Satan
and the wife of Job, wherein he explains to her that "you can have anything
in this world for money!"
[19]John Taylor, The Mediation and Atonement (Salt Lake City: Stevens
and Wallis, 1950), p. 70.

all the earth in glorious bloom, affords the Saints a holy home," and the situation is explained with perfect clarity in the 49th section of the Doctrine and Covenants, where we are told (1) that "the beasts of the field and the fowls of the air, and that which cometh of the earth, is ordained for the use of man for food and raiment, and that he might have abundance." We may take what we need, but (2) "wo be unto the man that sheddeth blood or that wasteth flesh and hath no need." We may not take more than we need. (3) Above all, we may not use this substance to exercise control and dominion over each other. "But it is not given that one man should possess that which is above another, wherefore the world lieth in sin." (D&C 49:19-21.) The sweeping indictment against the whole world gets down to fundamentals: Before the "blighting influence" of "inordinate appetite and love of this world . . . the strength, power, beauty, and glory that once adorned the form and constitution of many vanished away." (12:118:67.) Zion has ever been supplanted by Babylon, which is ever bent on converting the treasures of God's world into "the substance of an idol, which waxeth old, and shall perish in Babylon, even Babylon the great, which shall fall" (D&C 1:16); while with Zion the earth is to be "renewed and receive its paradisiacal glory."

The issue between the old and the new was drawn when Joseph Smith changed the up-and-coming name of Commerce, Illinois, to Nauvoo, "the Beautiful," and at Far West rebuked the speculators who would retain the techniques of Babylon in building Zion: "Brethren, we are gathered to this beautiful land to build up Zion. . . . But since I have been here I have perceived the spirit of selfishness. Covetousness exists in the hearts of the Saints. . . . Here are those beginning to spread out, buying up all the land they are able to, to the exclusion of the poorer ones who are not so much blessed with the world's goods, thinking to lay foundations for themselves, only looking to their individual families and those who are to follow them." Most Americans call this "vision," but

the Prophet Joseph had another word for it: "Now I want
to tell you that Zion cannot be built up in any such way. I
see signs put out, beer signs, speculative schemes are being
introduced. This is the way of the world, *Babylon* indeed,
and I tell you in the name of the God of Israel, if there is not
repentance . . . and a turning from such ungodliness, covetousness, and self-will you will be broken and scattered from
this choice land to the four winds of heaven."[20] Within a
short time this prophecy was fulfilled to the letter, and only
the faithful remnant of the Church went West.

What happened there? A generation later Brigham
Young addressed the conference of the Saints: "Have we
separated ourselves from the nations? Yes. And what else
have we done? Ask ourselves the question. Have we not
brought Babylon with us? Are we not promoting Babylon
in our midst? Are we not fostering the spirit of Babylon
that is now abroad on the face of the whole earth? I ask myself this question, and I answer, Yes, yes . . . we have too
much of Babylon in our midst." (17:38:74.) "One man has
his eye on a gold mine . . . another for selling his cattle . . .
another to get a farm, or building here and there, and trading
and trafficking with each other just like Babylon. . . . Babylon is here, and we are following in the footsteps of the
inhabitants of the earth, who are in a perfect sea of confusion. Do you know this? You ought to, for there are none
of you but what see it daily." (Ibid., p. 41.)

And what has this to do with the environment? That
whole economy was based on seizing and selling the treasures
of the earth beyond one's own personal needs—the land
itself, the minerals, water, soil, forests, grass—all are converted into means of making or purchasing the long list of
unnecessary wares that John the Revelator sets forth as
the quintessence of Babylon, whose "merchants are the great
men of the earth." (Revelation 18.) In the process their

        [20]Edward Stevenson, *Autobiography* (Microfilm in Church Historian's
Office), pp. 40-41, quoted by J. Grant Stevenson in *The Life of Edward
Stevenson* (master's thesis, BYU, 1955), p. 43.

beauty and value are destroyed, the short-lived finished product soon joining the earlier industrial wastes to cumber the earth with refuse. Why are we so foolish? For the same reason the Nephites were, because "Satan had great power . . . tempting them to seek for power, and authority, and riches, and the vain things of the world." (3 Ne. 6:15.) The "love of this world" is not an appreciation of the wonderful things that are in it, but the desire to possess it here and now, before we have shown that we can deal lovingly and wisely. The voice of Brother Brigham still pleads: "Do not obey the lusts of the flesh, the lusts of the eye, and the groveling grasping after property." (8:125:60.)

The history of America during the first hundred years of Mormonism was largely the history of the frontier, and most Americans still like to imagine themselves living in a land of inexhaustible resources in which everything is "up for grabs." Brigham Young exposed and denounced that myth from the beginning, though he recognized its powerful appeal: "We want to go where we can . . . mount our horses, and ride over the prairies, and say, I am Lord of all I survey . . . that we can get the whole world in a string after us, and have it all in our own possession by and by. . . . This is the object many have. . . . Elders of Israel are greedy after the things of this world." (1:164:53.) "Some want to be separated far from their neighbors, and own all the land around them, saying, 'All is right, all is peace.'" (1:107:53.) They simply are following the example of the Adversary, who gloried in his kingdom and his greatness where none dared molest or make afraid. But that illusion is not for the Saints: "Let us learn that the earth is not ours." (8:342:61.)

"Satan never owned the earth; he never made a particle of it; his labor is not to create, but to destroy." (10:320:64.) Yet it is he who puts it all up for sale and thereby achieves his work of confusion and destruction: "The riches of the world are natural, and common to the human family, but who governs and controls them?" (1:268:53.) "The earth is here, and the fullness thereof is here. It was made for man; and one man was not made to trample his fellowman under his feet" through the possession of it. (19:46:77.) "Light, intelligence, good, that which is of God creates, fashions, forms, builds, brings into existence, beautifies, makes excellent, glorifies, extends, and increases." But that is not the easy road to power; it is easier to doubt than to believe, to tear down a pioneer monument than to restore it, to set a fire than to put one out, so that "that which is not of God burns, destroys, cuts down, ruins. Light and intelligence lead people to the fountain of truth; while the opposite principle says, 'Don't believe a word, don't do a thing; burn up and destroy.' " (13:241:70.) It is a fundamental maxim of the Jews that wherever Satan as Mastemah rules on earth "he induces men to sin against the birds, and beasts, and reptiles, and fish, and to devour one another's flesh."[21] And that when Israel and mankind sin, nature itself is thrown into confusion, so that the violent destructions that overtake the wicked are of their own making. (Moses 7:13.) Brigham illustrated this principle from his own experience, describing how those parts of the land from which the Saints had been driven have since become poor and unproductive, "desolate, forlorn, and forsaken." (MS 38:344:76.) In the end, as the wise rabbis saw, it is pollution that makes the earth uninhabitable: "When you completely defile the land," Israel is told, "then I will no longer dwell in it; and then before long *you* can no longer dwell in it!"[22] For Babylon is the city dump, "a hold of every foul spirit, a cage of every unclean and hateful bird." (Revelation 18:2.) And so the warning goes out, "Not many years hence they shall not be left to pollute mine heritage." (D&C 105:15.) "A scourge and judgment will be poured out upon the children of Zion; for shall the children of the kingdom pollute my holy land?" (D&C 84:58f.) The process goes on while Satan operates with "wealth . . . used out of its legiti-

---

[21]II Enoch 7:5-6; Book of Jubilees 7:24; 8.
[22]Sabbath, Fol. 33a:12-14.

mate channel" to "subvert every wholesome law of God and man." (10:3:62.)

But all is not lost.

> The Spirit of the Lord and the keys of the priesthood hold power over all animated beings. When Father Adam transgressed the law he did not fall at once from the presence of the Lord. . . . Men continued to sin and degenerate from generation to generation . . . during this time the earth and all creation groaned in sin, and enmity increased, and the lives of man and beast decreased. . . . In this dispensation the keys . . . will be restored, and we are to return to the favor of the Lord . . . cease hostility with the serpents and lay aside all enmity and treat all animals kindly. (*Brigham Young History*, Apr. 26, 1846.)

It is not too late to heed this wisest of counselors: "Let me love the world as He loves it, to make it beautiful, and glorify the name of my Father in heaven. It does not matter whether I or anybody else owns it, if we only work to beautify and make it glorious, it is all right." (2:308:55.)

Commitment
and
Life's Meaning

C. Terry Warner

C. TERRY WARNER is director of the Honors Program for Brigham Young University, an attainment that has capped a brief but distinguished career for this young leader. During his first year at BYU he was named professor of the year.

He graduated with highest honors in the Honors Program at BYU in 1963, and then completed his M.A. and Ph.D. degrees at Yale University in philosophy.

He is former chairman of the department of philosophy at BYU. During his university training he attained many honors, including the Edwin Hinckley Memorial Fellowship, the Danforth Graduate Fellowship, the Woodrow Wilson Graduate Fellowship, and the Sterling Fellowship, which is the highest award given by Yale University to a graduate student.

He served a mission for the Church to Great Britain, and was bishop of the New Haven, Connecticut, Ward. He now serves on the Church's teacher development committee.

His wife is the former Susan Lillywhite, and they have five children.

COMMITMENT
AND LIFE'S MEANING[1]

C. Terry Warner

Synoptic Introduction

*On wild trees the flowers are fragrant; on
cultivated trees, the fruits.*
                                    —Philostratus the Elder[2]

*My son, do not think lightly of the Lord's discipline,
nor lose heart when he corrects you;
for the Lord disciplines those whom he loves;
he lays the rod on every son whom he acknowledges.*

                        —David, in Proverbs; quoted by
                        Paul in his letter to the Hebrews[3]

If fruit-bearing trees were self-aware, would they con-
sent to being pruned? With limbs surging to sprout and
reach in natural directions, could they be persuaded by the
gardener's promises of increased fruitfulness and health? It
is doubtful that they could. Certainly human beings, the
creatures that *are* self-aware, seldom submit willingly to any
sort of pruning, in spite of needing it more desperately than
any tree. They are propelled through life by desires that,
like plants' impetus toward growth, press naturally for satisfaction; it is accordingly not easy to convince them of the
necessity for "pruning"—for denying themselves satisfactions—if their lives are to be meaningful and happy.

----

[1]I want to thank Dillon Inouye, Dennis Rasmussen, Dianne Higginson,
Sterling Van Wagenen, James Faulconer, and especially Arthur Henry King
for suggestions and responses that helped me write this paper.

[2]From *Stories of Heroes*, quoted in Søren Kierkegaard, *Repetition*
(Princeton: Princeton University Press, 1941), p. 2.

[3]Hebrews 12:5-6. (All New Testament quotations but one have been taken
from the New English version [Oxford and Cambridge, 1970].)

To some of the world's people, the suggestion that self-denial can promote happiness seems silly. After all, what men desire are the things they think will make them happy; hence, the suggestion means in effect that we should believe that it will make us happy to forego the things that we think will make us happy.[4] This is foolishness;[5] and so, it is contended, is self-denial.

These people are disastrously mistaken about the character of human life. They think that desires can be fed unselectively without jeopardizing fulfillment and happiness. This is not so; each of life's options, like a bud or an elongating branch, drains away resources from all the others—including promising tender new spiritual growths—unless it is cut off. A decision must therefore be made as to whether it is worth what it costs, which is either the pruning away of other options or else, if there is no pruning at all, a general reduction in the quality of all the fruit that one's endeavors will bear. (The latter alternative is the decision tacitly made by those who refuse to decide.) At each of life's forkings a decision is made, and good fruit survives and grows only insofar as the buds of lesser fruit are deliberately clipped away. Happiness, the taste of good fruit, is therefore not the natural privilege of the uncultivated personality. It is, at least in part, an achievement.

There are other more reflective people in the world who are not dubious about whether men *should* undergo pruning, but rather about whether they *can*. Although men are unique among living things in their capacity to reflect upon their natural desires and strivings and to find them in large part pathetically self-serving and insignificant, they continue in these desirings and strivings anyway. It is as if our anthropomorphic trees became "intellectually" convinced of pruning's worth and in spite of this persisted with undiminished

---

[4]See the concluding subsection of this essay for an explanation of why the suggestion appears unreasonable but in fact is not.

[5]Ayn Rand, author of *The Fountainhead* and *Atlas Shrugged*, would, I think, take this position.

vigor in growing willy-nilly. As we later shall show, men's self-awareness—their capacity for self-evaluation—is an absurdity in the light of their behavior, but with equal justification we can say that their behavior is absurd in the light of their self-awareness.

Whereas the unreflective people I mentioned are mistaken, these latter reflective people are simply ignorant. In the first place, few of them profess to know of any enterprise that is sure to be worth self-sacrifice. Self-pruning, to be profitable at all, must conform to a plan in which one wholeheartedly believes. But they believe in no such plan. What is more, they are often suspicious of the very idea of a commitment that involves self-sacrifice, however noble or lofty its object. This is simply because the people who appear to be committed may in fact be doing merely what they personally want to do, in which case their persistence would not be commitment at all. For even if their goal requires sacrifice of other satisfactions, it is, like any other personal purpose, essentially if subtly self-serving and so tainted with ultimate meaninglessness. Reflective and honest men would be satisfied, if at all, only with an object of commitment transcending everything they naturally desire—an object whose intrinsic worthiness could lend significance to the labors they consecrate to it. They could promote such an object not merely because they would want to, but because it would be right. For this reason, they would not be plagued with the suspicion that they behave and forbear as they do *because* they enjoy doing so, even though their actions and self-denials might frequently coincide with what they enjoy. Thus they would be liberated from the presentiment that their lives are absurd. For these and other reasons to be mentioned later, an object of commitment higher than self would have to originate with someone else—someone perfectly trusted— and would have to be received as a stewardship. It would have to be a gift.

In the second place, reflective people cannot honestly

say that receiving such a gift would really help them, for they, with justification, doubt the ability of human beings to completely prune away all competing allegiances. Men cannot on their own power fundamentally alter their wayward desires (there are overwhelming arguments against the supposition that they can). Indeed, they even find that overriding them is a formidable challenge, for such desires are like flabby muscles—they undermine their owner's efforts to improve them. A man with wayward desires is in the same predicament as men with certain kinds of emotional or mental illness—he has difficulty rectifying his problem because the very instrument required for the task is the one which is out of commission. Men need power from an external source if their desires are to be purified and the process of self-pruning carried out. Once again a gift or endowment is required.

Of course only a divine person could provide such a gift. If reflective secular men doubt the possibility of genuine happiness (and they do), it is partly because they disbelieve in this person or in his willingness to help. Pessimism about man and ultimately unhappiness are outgrowths of irreligion. What point is there to pruning if the fruit will perish anyway?

Goodness and its particular deliciousness—which we variously call "joy," "happiness," "fulfillment," and "a sense of the meaningfulness of life"—are partly achievements of the person and partly gifts or endowments from God. The achievement results from an irrevocable commitment to a proffered trust or stewardship and from faithful sacrifice of everything that is inimical to that trust. (As we shall see, the commitment must be irrevocable in order to qualify as commitment at all.) The gifts consist of the initial proffering of the stewardship, the Spirit's constant instructions concerning what to prune and what to nurture, the power to cut off limbs bearing the evil and all-too-beloved fruits that sap one's moral strength (including one's will to cut them off), and the joyous witness of God's Spirit that one has been true to the trust. Men are different from trees, for they carry out their own pruning. But they can neither begin nor proceed without these gifts.

In this essay I first explore the necessity and nature of commitment, concentrating on the contribution that men can make to their own salvation. Thereafter I present certain reasons why this contribution must remain eternally inadequate unless the commitment is made to the Savior, by whose "grace . . . we are saved, after all we can do."[6]

Natural Man, Commitment, and Life's Meaning

> God and the devil are fighting for mastery, and the battlefield is the heart of man.
>
> —Fyodor Dostoevsky[7]

> You say, "How rich I am! And how well I have done! I have everything I want." In fact, though you do not know it, you are the most pitiful wretch, poor, blind, and naked. . . . I know all your ways; that though you have a name for being alive, you are dead. Wake up, and put some strength into what is left, which must otherwise die!
>
> —The Lord to the Churches at Laodicea and Sardis[8]

> By faith Moses . . . considered the stigma that rests on God's Anointed greater wealth than the treasures of Egypt, for his eyes were fixed upon the coming day of recompense. . . . [H]e was resolute.
>
> —Paul to the Hebrews[9]

About the Term "Natural Man." In this section I shall discuss an attitude, endemic in modern literature,[10] of sensitive secular men who have not found, or at least have not

---

[6]2 Nephi 25:23. Cf. 2 Corinthians 12:9; Doctrine and Covenants 17:8; Ether 12:27.

[7]Fyodor Dostoevsky, *The Brothers Karamozov*, tr. David Magarshack, 2 vols. (Harmondsworth, Mddx. Penguin Books, 1958), vol. 1, p. 124.

[8]Revelation 3:17, 1-2.

[9]Hebrews 11:26-27.

[10]See for example the so-called "existentialist" literature of contemporary Europe, e.g., Albert Camus' *The Myth of Sysiphus* and *The Stranger*.

embraced, any object of commitment that transcends their own, merely personal desires. This is the attitude expressed by Hamlet: "How weary, stale, flat, and unprofitable seem . . . all the uses of this world."[11] My contention will be that there is a connection between lack of commitment, on one hand, and, on the other, this inability to see significance and to find joy in life.

Though my remarks will be couched in a largely secular terminology, I want to introduce one key scriptural term in order to make the discussion maximally illuminating. The term is *natural man*.[12] I shall not attempt a precise theological definition of this term, but indicate merely that in the scriptures it seems among other things to connote such characteristics of the "normal" human being as selfishness, greed, pride, indulgence, self-deception[13]—characteristics that may not be particularly destructive in most of us, and which are in general partially offset by many unegoistic aspirations, but which must be obliterated from any personality that becomes godlike.[14] In other words, I shall apply the term *natural man* to those standing in need of repentance and of the purifying and enlivening power of the redemption. And I shall suggest that irrevocable commitment to something transcending self is part (but only part) of the process by which the "normal" self-involved tendencies and dispositions to sin,[15] which distinguish us from the Savior, are purged from us.[16]

---

[11]*Hamlet,* Act I, scene II.

[12]See, e.g., Alma 41:11; Mosiah 3:21; Romans 8:7; Alma 42:10.

[13]See the interesting statement of C. S. Lewis in *The Four Loves* (London: Collins, 1960), p. 53.

[14]Mosiah 27:25; cf. David O. McKay's remarkable letter to his son on the atonement, dated December 20, 1920, *Treasures of Life* (Salt Lake City: Deseret Book Company, 1962), pp. 275-78; also his speech given at BYU October 12, 1962, "Something Higher Than Self" (BYU Extension Publications 1965).

[15]Mosiah 5:2; Alma 19:33; 2 Corinthians 5:17; Galatians 2:20; Romans 6:4; Romans 6:11.

[16]The natural man doctrine has been controversial. Some, supposing it to mean that men are essentially evil, or depraved, have called it pessimistic. But it means no such thing: men are innocent as children and may again become innocent through repentance and the redemptive power manifest

I shall in what follows frequently refer to the "natural man" and occasionally to the complementary type, the "spiritual man." It should be understood that these are not actual men but types—"ideal types," if you will. They are paradigms, not necessarily found exemplified in life, that actual individuals approximate more or less closely. Such types or paradigms are appropriately used as guidelines for understanding individuals but not as descriptions of them; the individuals themselves differ widely in respect of their "natural" and "spiritual" qualities and indeed possess various combinations of both. And insofar as they have become spiritual, I would maintain, they have done so only by conforming to the principles of the gospel.

The Meaninglessness of the Natural Life. Each successive moment finds the natural man seeking satisfaction of one of his desires (or placation of one of his fears). But satisfaction (or placation) does not content him. Though he feels that getting the promotion, winning the damsel, or becoming a star will bring him happiness at last, he no sooner possesses the object of his striving than it loses its attractiveness for him and he begins to yearn for something further.

---

through priesthood ordinances. The doctrine is pessimistic only to those who disbelieve in this power.

From the fact that men's natures require God's transformation, it follows that they would come to no good end without him, but it does not follow from this necessity for grace that they are essentially evil. That grace is a condition for salvation does not mean that it is a sufficient condition. It is in fact only a necessary one—there is much that men must and can do also. Men's responsiveness to righteous opportunities is also a necessary condition, from whence it follows that, rather than being essentially either good or evil, men as such have potential for goodness and godliness, evil and devilry, and every condition in between. The very (and very tiresome) question "Are men basically good or evil?" must be rejected. Both possible answers are false. The question presupposes that either man's moral resources are sufficient to make human society a Camelot or that God will unilaterally make it such. But in fact neither supposition is true. The question rests on a simple confusion of necessary and sufficient conditions.

While acknowledging this much goodness in men—sufficient goodness to enable them to respond to divine appeal and receive divine power for the sanctification of their natures—it is also imperative to remember that they cannot save themselves. Though most of them are good relative to the evil of which they are capable, they are something much less than that relative to the good of which they are capable. People who, while acknowledging that there is goodness in men, overlook the difference between that attained good-

He is driven on by the prospect that gratification will fulfill him, but he is in fact incapable of fulfillment.[17]

Why cannot satisfaction of selfish and carnal desires fulfill him? The answer is to be found in the fact that, as a man rather than some other member of the animal kingdom, he can "step back" from his engagements in his world and take a spectator's perspective on them—he can view them, as it is said, *sub specie aeternitatis*. And when he does this, he is beset by the awareness that his aims and strivings are petty or pointless; that in a world in which, as all his intuitions tell him, there ought to be significant things to do, his preoccupation with titillating and indulging a few pounds of flesh seems ludicrous indeed.[18]

This preoccupation will strike him not only as pathetic but also as smacking of absurdity. The reason is that he is apparently serious about the objects of his strivings and at the same time finds it impossible to take those strivings se-

---

[17]Arthur Shoepenhauer's brilliant exposition of this view is widely known. In summarizing it, Harold Hoeffding says: "The only positive feelings are those of pain; it is in them that the unceasing desire and the unceasing lust which preserve and carry on life make themselves felt. Each time that this inner fire is for the moment quenched by the satisfaction of desire a feeling of pleasure arises, but the nature of this feeling is essentially negative since it only supplies a want. We are the dupes of an illusion when it appears to us a positive condition." *A History of Modern Philosophy*, vol. 2 (Dover Publications), p. 231-32.

[18]Those interested may want to consult Hume's poignantly bleak observations on human life, e.g., *Dialogues Concerning Natural Religion*, Part X, and *A Treatise of Human Nature*, Book I, Part 4, Section 7.

---

ness and the righteousness that the Savior exemplifies and that they have yet to attain, tend to lose sight of their spiritual needs, including their need for the transforming power of the Redeemer. Moreover, they are left with bleak belief, whether they like it or not, that the kind of society we have now is about the best we can hope for. It is this humanism that I, for one, find pessimistic, not the natural man doctrine with its intimate connection with the prospect of redemption. With this pessimism as the alternative, it is clear that believing in the possibility of men's moral improvement is scarcely a disparagement of them, even if it is added that they cannot be radically improved without help.

There is a curious twist in the discussion over the natural man (NM) doctrine. Its opponents find it pessimistic, for they characteristically de-emphasize the necessity for rebirth and redemption, without which process NM is a gloomy doctrine indeed (see Alma 42:11). Against such pessimism they cite the optimistic doctrine that men have a divine potential (DP). What is curious is that DP, taken together with a few unexceptionable theological and empirical facts, actually entails NM. Thus NM's opponents who appeal to

riously as he contemplates them under the aspect of eternity.[19] The objects matter; their mattering does not.[20] And so in
spite of his capacity for self-transcendence, which marks him
off from the rest of the animals, allowing him to evaluate his
goals and strivings and to find them petty and selfish, he,
creature of desire and victim of the moment that he is, persists in his self-serving ways just as other animals do. The
man's doubts about the animal's strivings do not alter them,
and therefore his uniquely human capacity for self-evaluation is reduced at best to a useless burden and at worst to a
guilt-generating device for calculating, multiplying, and refining selfish satisfactions and hence for making them even
more touchingly gratuitous in his eyes. All of this makes
the fact that he is a man, rather than an unreflective animal,
absurd.

Reflective self-awareness, even if merely vague, only
serves to drive most men back in premonitional terror to their
prereflective projects. The natural man lets himself be caught

---

[19]Thomas Nagel offers this point in explanation of the sense that men
(in my vocabulary, men in the state of nature) have that life is absurd; my
explanation, given a few sentences later, is slightly different. See "The Absurd,"
Journal of Philosophy 68 (1971). Although his paper appeared when this one
was entering its final draft, it confirmed my ideas and in one instance helped
me crystallize them. As will be obvious in the latter part of the present paper,
I believe his conclusions that the sense of life's absurdity is universal, because
grounded in the character of man as such, is in error; in my view, this sense
is grounded in the character of the natural man. His conclusion is incompatible
with the reality of the redemption--which he, of course, does not accept. But
he and I would agree that in spite of individuals' hopes, protestations, and even
convictions to the contrary, life is ultimately absurd if there is no redeeming
Christ; the difference between us is that I affirm and he (I presume) denies
that a Redeemer exists.

[20]Perhaps there is no more poignant passage in literature illustrating this
than Mormon 2:14: "And they did not come unto Jesus with broken hearts
and contrite spirits, but they did curse God, and wish to die. Nevertheless they
would struggle with the sword for their lives."

DP are forced on logical grounds to accept NM, and when combined with
the disbelief in the redemption with which they started, this is the very
pessimism that they sought to escape in the first place!

That DP, together with a few innocuous premises, entails NM is seen as
follows:

1. God is pure.
2. DP: men can eventually be like God in repect of purity (1 John 3:2).
3. If they are like God in this respect now, then he is like them in this
   respect now.

up in business or competition or diverted by drink or gossip
in order to evade the empty feeling he has when not indulging some illusory hope or diversion. He rarely awakens to
the fact that the objects of his striving—possessions, con-
quests, pleasures, and comforts—bring no happiness because,
in spite of what he may tell himself, he is not precisely seeking happiness. What he is seeking is protection and escape
from the realization that he is only a creature of the moment,
subjugated—nay, driven—by desires and fears that he cannot respect, and that the perennial content of his mind and
heart is as impermanent and insignificant as the objects from
which it is borrowed. This is why he seldom engages in activities that will suggest to him the pathos of his condition—
for instance, introspection and prayer—but instead in whatever seems titillating or diverting, whatever will take the
"curse" off the moment. When he does not succeed in finding something to this purpose, he feels empty, bored, and dis-
contented; and when he does succeed, he is only preoccupied
temporarily—he is on a pendulum swinging between empti-
ness and diversion.

For all these reasons, such seriousness as a reflective natural man has about his activities is at best forced, for it is
perpetually troubled by the repressed awareness that it is designed to block out and perpetually undermined by a more
fundamental attitude, that of frivolity or lightmindedness.
He may try romantically to plunge so wholeheartedly into a
project as to make it meaningful by force of will, but he
knows deep down that his effort is desperate and that he
does not believe in it. When all the masks and scaffolding of
his life are stripped away, he cannot believe that his projects
matter—petty aims deserve frivolous attitudes. Surprising

---

4. But he is not like them in this respect now (he does not, for example,
   have men's moral weaknesses).
5. (Hence, men are not now like God in respect of purity (this follows
   from 3 and 4), and this is, at least in part, what the scriptures mean
   by saying men are "in a state of nature."

Again, any man disbelieving in the necessity for redemption and rebirth but
believing in DP cannot avoid a profoundly pessimistic form of NM, no matter
how he may prefer to suppose that man is basically good.

though it may be, the truth is that a deep-lying frivolity commonly goes hand in hand with the artificial earnestness that accompanies self-evasion, and both are the bedfellows of despair. No wonder that a thoughtful contemporary man characteristically feels that, like everything else in his ambit of concern, for him to exist does not really matter. It does not even matter that nothing matters. Along with everything else, contemplation loses its point, and there is no good reason to be found for doing anything—except, of course, whatever will quell the anxiety of this very awareness that nothing matters.

The life of this kind of person breaks up psychologically into unconnected momentary fragments. Nothing gives its moments meaning beyond the ephemeral significance they possess as mere passing portions of time; nothing binds them together as part of a single unified life. Wrote Søren Kierkegaard: "For if passion continues in a man, it changes his life into nothing but instants and as passion cunnningly serves its deluded master, it gradually gains the ascendency until the master serves it like a blind serf!"[21] Sensing his lack of control over the aims to which his behavior is constantly dedicated, the natural man may be struck by the not uncommon thought that perhaps he may be nothing more than a succession of momentary bodily and psychical responses. Indeed, as he thinks upon the matter, he realizes that he has no sense of self, no identity as a person. There is no continuous thread running through his states and binding them together that he can call "me."

These anxiety reactions of the natural man when he reflects upon the meaning of his life are common psychological phenomena. Even when such a man avoids reflecting on his life, the loss of self and meaninglessness of life are nevertheless there waiting to be acknowledged and, in the meantime, literally driving him to distraction.

_____

[21]*Purity of Heart Is to Will One Thing*, trans. Douglas V. Steere (New York: Harper and Brothers Publishers, 1938), p. 51.

Commitment and the Meaning of Life.   Men are not doomed to labor in this condition; they can integrate and thus make meaningful the discrete moments of their lives. This they can do by irrevocably committing themselves and remaining faithful to an enterprise transcending these moments and their portent of fleeting satisfactions. (In this too men are unlike animals. "Man," said Nietzsche, "is the only being who makes promises."[22]) Commitment is different from mere reflective condenmnation of one's natural desires. Fixed upon something beyond the desires, it can give an individual leverage against them so that he does not have to yield to them.

When this happens, the attractions and enticements of the moment cease to fill his consciousness, distracting him from things that matter. No longer all-important, they now subserve a higher end, and the moments they occupy become bound together with other moments in a unified pathway leading through time toward an envisioned goal. And without being sought directly, a sense of selfhood appears. It is an exhilarating sense of self-control whereby one can shape his responses to his circumstances, pruning away the forbidden ones at will and so fashioning his own character. It is the sense of having an identity transcending and running through the moments of time. But without commitment, the discrete states of the person cannot be endowed with an overarching meaning, and the man remains psychologically unintegrated.

The meaningfulness of a committed life is due partly to the fact that the capacity to appreciate, enjoy, and value people and experiences is tied to one's willingness to sacrifice whatever is inimical to acting righteously. Charity "seeketh not her own."[23] Alma told his son Shiblon that if he would sacrifice wholesale gratification of appetites and passions, he would increase in this capacity; other people would *by that*

---

[22]Quoted in Gabriel Marcel, *Being and Having: An Existentialist Diary,* trans, Katherine Farrer (New York: Harper and Row, 1965), p. 14.
[23]Moroni 7:45.

very means become more significant to him. His words: "See that ye bridle all your passions, that ye may be filled with love."[24]

Thus, on the principle of *sacrifice*—of giving up willingly whatever is extraneous to the object of commitment—a man can make his life meaningful. He forges a self only by sacrificing whatever is self-serving (that is, by what is called "self-sacrificing"—by committing himself to something higher than himself).

Now the object of genuine commitment (1) is not an object of self-serving desires, (2) is a desire to do what is right, (3) is given by another person, and (4) that other person is divine. We have already considered reasons why some of these conditions obtain; let us amplify and add to these reasons.

We can do this best by considering how the natural man, just insofar as he is a natural man, is incapable of commitment and faithfulness. Though he can persist in an activity, even sacrificing some satisfactions in order to have others more to his liking (or lusting), this persistence is hardly commitment.

First, the natural man's striving is not commitment or faithfulness because the desire that motivates it is subject to change.[25] If something new strikes his fancy tomorrow—some more attractive or exciting person than his spouse or more rewarding opportunity than one he has promised to fulfill—he will alter his course. Since he cannot guarantee in advance what he will desire the next day (desires being subject to change independently of the will), he cannot honestly say that he is committed or that he in any way stands apart from and above his momentary physiological and psychological states. For this reason, it approaches a contradiction in terms to say that a man can be faithful in pursuing selfish goals.

------

[24]Alma 38:12.
[25]Cf. Marcel, op. cit., pp. 41-42.

These considerations make it easy to see why having an eye *single* to the glory of God and taking upon oneself the Savior's name with *full* purpose of heart[26] cannot be motivated naturally and selfishly. Kierkegaard pointed out that whereas purity of heart is to will one thing, no object except the will of God (= the Good) can be a single thing. All other things are subject to continual change, as is the desire to have or enjoy them. The result is that the natural man pitches upon lust and lists upon satiation and disappointment. He is double-minded, as James says, "unstable in all his ways"[27] and "at odds with himself."[28]

Second, precisely because the natural man's purposes are his own, their worth is tinged with doubt. This is true no matter how dignified the purposes, whether they be justice, knowledge, virtue, conquest, or wealth. The point is a subtle and philosophical one that might be explained as follows: A man's genuine commitment obliges him to act in certain appropriate ways and thereby renders him responsible for so acting. From this it follows that the object of commitment cannot be the object of his natural desires as a fallen being, for it makes no sense to say that one is committed to, obliged to, and responsible for doing what he already wants to do anyway and indeed *will* do if unimpeded. In such a case, there is always the suspicion that the so-called commitment is extraneous; that the agent acts not because of the commitment but because he wants to. As mentioned earlier, the actions that commitment requires of a person might well coincide with what he finds enjoyable to do, and in performing them he might well enjoy them. But the prospect of enjoying what he does is not its cause, for he would act the same way even if he thought he would not enjoy doing so. He acts as he does because of his commitment.

If one cannot be committed to doing one's own will,

---

[26]Matthew 6:22 and 2 Nephi 31:13; cf. Mosiah 7:33, Doctrine and Covenants 88:67, and Mormon 8:15.
[27]James 1:8; cf. James 4:8 and Matthew 6:24.
[28]Kierkegaard, op. cit., p. 56.

commitment is possible only if its object is doing the will of another. Only if the aims of one's life are given to him, only if he is responsible to another by whom they are given, can he be obligated at all and deny himself at all. One can only be responsible in responsiveness to another. In a passage that inspired this essay, Gabriel Marcel wrote:

> Fidelity, unless it is to be fruitless or, worse, reduced to mere persistency, must spring from something that is "absolutely given" to me . . . . From the very beginning there must be a sense of stewardship: something has been entrusted to us, so that we are not only responsible towards ourselves, but towards an active and superior principle. . . . There is no commitment purely from my own side; it always implies that the other being has a hold over me. All commitment is a response. . . . As I see it, and despite appearances to the contrary, fidelity is never fidelity to one's self, but is referred to what I called the hold the other being has over us.[29]

Third, I may appear to be saying that the object of true commitment is not something one desires. If so, it will quite naturally be objected that this claim is implausible. For if the tree consents to its own pruning, it must find pruning worthwhile—more worthwhile than avoiding the pain it will cause. It would make no sense to say that the object of commitment is not an object of desire.

And indeed it does make no sense to say this. But it does make sense to say that the desire that motivates commitment is of a kind fundamentally different from the desires that characterize the natural man. In the former case, things are desired because they are right; in the latter, because they are somehow advantageous to the individual. Thus, instead of saying that men act contrary to *all* desire, which is implausible, I am saying that there is a duality of kinds of desire in them. If there were not, they could not transcend their natural selves—they would not even desire to do so; they could at best only desire some selfishly advantageous ends in preference to others. And in this case, I maintain, genuine

---

[29]Marcel, op. cit., pp. 14-15, 46.

commitment would be impossible. Kant discovered long ago[30] that morality is possible only if man is a dual creature: only if there is something in him besides his carnal and selfish nature can he overcome that nature.

Fourth, later I shall suggest that only those acts of commitment that are fixed upon doing the Savior's will perfectly fit Marcel's description. You may object that service to other people does also—by putting others' purposes before one's own, one could genuinely deny himself and so transcend his selfishness. There is a measure of truth in this. Insofar as such service is motivated by an appreciation of its rightness rather than any advantage that might be gained from it, it can yield a certain amount of genuine happiness. But where the issue is whether there can be any *ultimate* significance given to human life, the objection runs aground upon a tough question. If one's strivings as a natural man are absurd, how can it be any less absurd to promote someone else's? Later I shall indicate how one can avoid this pitfall in service to others that is rendered via obedience to the Savior.

But how then, you may ask, can natural men find within theselves the wherewithal to commit themselves irrevocably to something higher than themselves? How can they extricate themselves from the motivational momentum that has them in its thrall? The answer can only be that they do not lift themselves up by their own corrupted bootstraps but struggle up with the assistance of an uncorrupted Hand. As we have already seen, the ascendency of man is a corporate project. The individual is divinely empowered to subdue the resistance within him when he responds with immovable determination to the Lord's appeal to his spirit. These conditions governing the process of putting off the natural man constitute yet another reason why commitment, to be worthy of the name, must center in the will of Another and begin in response to that will.

------

[30]See John Silber, "The Copernican Revolution in Ethics: The Good Reexamined," *Kant-Studien* (Köln: Kölner Universitätsverlag), 51:85-101 (1959-60).

Freedom and Self-Creation. Typically the natural man has avoided all commitments because he has not wanted to bind himself to anything; he has supposed that doing so would jeopardize his freedom. But he finds that just because he is unconditionally committed to nothing, he has no self capable of being free. Moreover, since he is incapable of being gratified, there is nothing he really prizes or values that he is free to enjoy. And finally he is enslaved by his desires—he is, as the scripture says, "in the bonds of iniquity."[31] He has sacrificed nothing in hopes of remaining free to have everything, only to discover that he has lost his freedom and is capable of enjoying nothing at all.

Contrast this with the man who has committed himself to something independent of his carnal desiring. This is the man who will never allow inconvenience or disinclination to keep him from fulfilling his word. He sacrifices much that he wants—wants indeed as badly as the selfish man— because he is determined not to be faithless. It is his having voluntarily bound himself to something higher than himself that liberates this sort of man from selfishness. Besides being free, he is also transformed, for the former natural fellow who walked in his shoes ceases to live as such.[32]

There are philosophical grounds for these theological points. Consider the following line of reasoning. A particular thing is the kind of thing it is because of the laws to which its behavior conforms. For instance, the object that I see in the sky is a bird, not primarily because of its appearance— decoys can share that appearance—but rather because it flies in graceful curvilinear patterns. As one philosopher pointed out, seeing that it is a bird "involves seeing that it will not suddenly do vertical snap rolls; and this is more than" mere appearance.[33] By the same token, if it *were* to do vertical snap rolls, we would immediately conclude that it was some sort

---

[31]Alma 41:11; cf. John 8:34 and Mosiah 27:29.
[32]Romans 6:6-7.
[33]Norwood Russell Hanson, *Patterns of Discovery* (Cambridge: University Press, 1961), p. 21.

of disguised mechanical device. The same is true of trees, rocks, grass, and everything in our world—they are what they are because of the laws to which their behavior conforms.

Now unlike birds, rocks, and grass, men are subject to *two* kinds of law. First, there are laws of nature such as gravity, Newton's laws, the drive for survival, and so on. These are laws that make men part of the animal kingdom; ordinarily they are laws that one does not choose to break or obey. We call them "descriptive laws." Besides these there are "prescriptive laws," man-made or God-given, that we can either break or obey. The possibility of abiding by prescriptive laws means that men can become different creatures than they would otherwise be. By voluntarily conforming to higher laws, they become more intricately organized and participate in a higher form of life. In this connection a statement of C. S. Peirce is interesting:

> Man comes from the womb in actuality an animal little higher than a fish; by no means as high as a serpent. His humanity consists in his *destination*. He becomes not actual man until he acquires self-control and then he is so in the measure of his self-control.[34]

To the degree that men control themselves in order to conform to God's laws, they become more nearly divine beings, for these laws in their fulness define what it is to be a god. "And . . . that which is governed by law is also preserved by law and perfected and sanctified by the same."[35]

It may not be extreme to say that by intensely striving to conform to the law and pattern given of God, a man may participate in his own creation as new and spiritual man. Certainly it is only in obedience to prescriptive laws of God that men, abetted by his power, can achieve leverage against and break the hold of descriptive laws that heretofore have defined them as natural men. It is precisely for this reason

---

[34]Charles Sanders Peirce, "The Argument for Pragmatism Anachagomenally or Recessively Stated," unpublished manuscript in the Harvard University archives.
[35]Doctrine and Covenants 88:34.

that only in obedience can men become free. As Elder Boyd K. Packer put it, we are liberated from the tyranny of Satan and sin in that act in which we say to God, "I do not want to do what I want to do. I want to do what thou wouldst have me do."[36]

Commitment Writ Large

I have been contrasting two fundamental attitudes that a man may take toward life. These are the same two attitudes that can be be taken toward a marriage and a community. It may shed light on my thesis concerning the individual life to consider these attitudes in the context of human relations. The natural man's attitude toward marriage is expressed in the statement, "Let's see how it works out." The attitude of the committed man is expressed in the statement, "How am I going to make it work out?"

Given the first attitude, it is *impossible* for a marriage to succeed. The moments of marriage are then no more meaningful than the moments of a natural man's life—not because the two partners "are not right for each other," but because by their attitude they declare that they are self-seeking and that therefore what has value for them is not the marriage as such but what they can individually get from it. They do not constitute a union, but a mere aggregate of thieving competitors fallen together to take from one another as long as it remains advantageous to do so.[37] It is known at the outset that they will bail out when it suits them; consequently, defensive measures are taken in advance to protect against rejection. Therefore, what passes for love in this relationship is at the very best a medium of barter or exchange. Self-defensive, the individuals do not venture the capital of fellow-feeling unless collateral is secured. The spirit of their transactions is "I will love you if you will love

---

[36]Boyd K. Packer in a devotional address at Brigham Young University December 7, 1971.

[37]Cf. Robert Graves' poem "The Thieves" in Robert Graves, *Poems Selected by Himself* (London: Penguin Books, 1957), p. 139.

me." A marriage? No, a market place when things go well; an adversary proceeding when they do not.

The principles of such a liaison can no more give it a meaning that transcends their individual selfish aims than the natural man can give unity to his life. Fidelity in marriage is but a species of the fidelity that is required to give meaning to life. (And that is why the notion of trial marriage is a joke—or would be if it were not fraught with tragic implications. The term "trial marriage" is as near a contradiction in terms as "selfish faithfulness.")

Denis de Rougemont maintained just this: Fidelity alone creates a human personality, for, he argued, the personality is built up or created in precisely the way that things are made, and that is by fidelity of the maker to a vision or pattern of something that does not yet exist. "Person, made thing, fidelity—the three terms are neither separable nor separately intelligible. All three presuppose *that a stand has been taken,* and that we have adopted what is fundamentally the attitude of creators." Likening the creation of an individual personality to the making of a marriage, he wrote, "The pledge exchanged in marriage is the very type of *serious* act, because it is a pledge given once and for all. The irrevocable alone is serious."[38]

"The irrevocable alone is serious." A man might with profit meditate for weeks on such a sentence. For the subject of marriage, it implies that only the man freely bound by covenant to his union with his bride can grow to care profoundly for her. Love is not a happy synchrony of heartbeats, nor marriage a lucky complementarity of selfish purposes—both are, in part, achievements and as such require fidelity to what can be but is not yet.

What is true of marriage is true of a community, however large or small. Arranged as a harmonious confluence of individual inclinations, it can never become a Camelot. Neither security nor permanence can obtain when each knows

----

[38]Denis de Rougemant, *Love in the Western World,* 2d ed. (New York: Pantheon Books, 1956), p. 308.

that the others' acceptance of him and of their societal relationships is ultimately grounded in enlightened self-interest.
As in marriage, that knowledge forces each one to protect
himself against the possibility that someday his welfare may
run counter to the others' interest. The extremity of this
situation, which more closely approaches the further the
majority fall into a state of nature, was well described by
Hobbes as a war of all against all in which life is "solitary,
poor, nasty, brutish, and short."[39] (If you do not believe it,
read a detailed history of war and plunder or review again
the agonizing battlefield tales in Mormon and Ether.)[40] In
less extreme forms, it seems to me to offer all the satisfactions available in a city of pickpockets who keep their
wallets sewn to their underwear. Without irrevocable covenants, groups may exist but not communities.

These considerations help one appreciate the "immutable
and unchangeable" promises and freely-subscribed-to covenants between the Lord and each steward upon which Zion
is founded.[41] They indicate to one the source of the power behind the School of the Prophets, in which the appointed
teacher would with uplifted hands salute the school members
as they entered with these words:

> Art thou a brother or brethren? I salute you in the name of
> the Lord Jesus Christ, in token or remembrance of the everlasting cov-
> enant, in which I will receive you to fellowship, in a determination that is
> fixed, immovable, and unchangeable, to be your friend and brother
> through the grace of God in the bonds of love, to walk in all the com-
> mandments of God blameless, in thanksgiving, forever and ever. Amen.[42]

I have indicated why there will never be peace among
natural men who merely follow their inclinations—they are
incapable of loving one another. And I have suggested why,
by fixedly, immovably, and unchangeably determining in the

[39]Thomas Hobbes, *Leviathan*, chap. 13.
[40]Mormon 2-6 and Ether 7-15.
[41]Doctrine and Covenants 104.
[42]Doctrine and Covenants 82:10.

brotherhood of the Lord to love one another, they will find that, with the regenerative power of the priesthood ordinances operative in them, they can become capable of mutual love. In society as in marriage, love is not among the natural man's repertoire of basic attitudes—it is, in part, an achievement.

Commitment to the Savior

In brief space mortals'
delight is exalted, and thus again it drops to the ground,
shaken by a backward doom.

We are the things of a day. What are we? What are we
    not? The shadow of a dream
is man, no more. *But when the brightness comes, and
    God gives it,
there is a shining of light on men, and there life is sweet.*
                                                        —Pindar[43]

And what of ourselves? With all these witnesses to faith around us like a cloud, we must throw off every encumbrance, every sin to which we cling, and run with resolution the race for which we are entered, our eyes fixed on Jesus, on whom faith depends from start to finish: Jesus who, for the sake of the joy that lay ahead of him, endured the cross, making light of its disgrace, and has taken his seat at the right hand of the throne of God.
                                                —Paul to the Hebrews[44]

Whether a commitment to something higher than self has sustaining power so that it can give an inexhaustible meaning to life at any and every stage of a person's development depends not only upon the perfectness of his fidelity but also upon the nature of the object to which he is committed. And it is because of the nature of its object that faithfulness to the Savior is the only way that men can integrate their personalities and make their lives fully significant. Consider these points.

---

[43]*The Odes of Pindar,* trans. Richmond Lattimore (Chicago: University of Chicago Press, 1947), p. 80. Italics added.
[44]Hebrews 12:1-2.

1. The Savior alone has power to purge us of the inner enemy, our impure desires, that threatens to undermine our commitment and thereby reintroduce the absurdity of life in a natural state. Only in him, therefore, can we be certain that the commitment can be carried through. The importance of this point cannot be exaggerated.

2. Hence, we will not, as we approach him more closely, find previously unsuspected reasons to disbelieve in our power to keep our commitment.

3. Any object that we pursue for self-serving reasons can be jeopardized, and this means that we cannot be sure we will not in some future moment stoop to immorality to protect or preserve our treasure. The will of the Savior is the only will that *always* dictates what is morally right to do.

4. Other objects of commitment besides the Savior's will may disappoint us as we approach them more closely. Wrote T. E. Lawrence, who, as he himself said, made or played with kings and prime ministers, "Anyone who had gone up so fast as I went and had seen so much of the inside of the top of the world might well lose his aspirations, and get weary of the ordinary motives of action, which had moved him until he reached the top."[45]

5. Closely allied with this is the fact that the Savior's love, which enticed us to venture in the first place, will not change as we strive to serve. Even if nothing else is constant in the universe, that love is.

6. Nor will our love wane as we, growing progressively more pure and more capable of love, taste more of his.

7. He makes commitments in return ("I, the Lord, am bound when ye do what I say"); hence, there is surety of reward for our consecration and hope.

8. One of the rewards is his approbation, expressed joyously in us by the Spirit's witness that we have been faithful in our stewardships. Paul wrote to the Romans:

---

[45]T. E. Lawrence, Letter to Ernest Thurtle, *The Letters of T. E. Lawrence of Arabia*, ed. David Garnett (London: Jonathan Cape, 1938), p. 653.

Let us exult in the hope of the divine splendor that is to be ours. More than this: let us even exult in our present sufferings, because we know that suffering trains us to endure, and endurance brings proof that we have stood the test, and this proof is the ground of hope. Such a hope is no mockery, because God's love has flooded our inmost heart through the Holy Spirit he has given us.[46]

9. Commitment to any code or creed or master plan for men, or indeed any abstract principle, might well destroy a man. For one thing (and this is but a negative expression of the first point), by the law alone he cannot be transformed, but only condemned for his inability to abide it. "The letter killeth."

Why let people dictate to you: "Do not handle this, do not taste that, do not touch the other"—all of them things that must perish as soon as they are used? That is to follow merely human injunctions and teaching. True, it has an air of wisdom, with its forced piety, its self-mortification and its severity to the body; but it is of no use at all in combating sensuality.[47]

Second, what a man in his imperfect understanding conceives at any given time will be incomplete or mistaken.[48] And because he relies too heavily upon this imperfect conception of what is good, he will tend at some point to be unteachable—perhaps even to the extent of ignoring the Spirit at some critical juncture of his life in favor of the abstraction upon which his mind, as well as his heart, is fixed. Thus did the Pharisees repeatedly claim to find fault with the Lord by appealing to the very law of which he was the author.

But if it is primarily upon a holy Person that one's heart is fixed, instead of upon a set of propositions (however "orthodox" they may appear), his commitment can be absolute without causing a premature closure of his conception of the truth. How this can be is seen when we contemplate what a thing of wonder is the fact that "the way, the

---

[46]Romans 5:2-5.
[47]Colossians 2:21-23.
[48]See Doctrine and Covenants 58:3.

truth, and the life"[49] is a Being full of love for us rather than a set of propositions carved austerely in stone. How else, except by being primarily committed, not to an ideology but to its source, can men cherish the truth instead of merely their conception of it and so remain teachable?

10. There is another aspect of Pharisaism that can be avoided by allegiance to a perfect loving Person. I refer to a general loss of openness and sensitivity that accompanies the judgmental attitude characteristic of the man whose mind is fixed upon principles alone. He pastes labels on everything instantaneously; he sizes people up before getting to know them. In these and other ways, he renders his world sterile, extinguishes his own sense of wonder, and forfeits the child-likeness and ingenuousness that the Savior has enjoined him to preserve—or recapture. Because people tend to go out of focus for him—he sees them not as individuals but as label-wearers, measuring them condemnatorily against the ideology to which he is committed—he is unloving. Historically religionists of his ilk, as inquisitors and as crusaders, have given religion a bad name.

As I see it, only allegiance to a divine Person can immunize one against this syndrome. Some people attempt to avoid it by emphasizing love at the expense of all commitments, but we have already seen that a man's capacity to care profoundly wanes when his commitment does. And we have seen that commitment to an abstraction also makes a man unloving. Hence, for a man to be unloving, he must (a) be committed and, what is more, (b) be committed to a loving and perfectly trustworthy Person. When and only when these conditions obtain, can he have uncompromisingly strong ideals and principles without scorning, if ever so subtly, those who do not share them, for, he is aware, the very medium in which he has received them is the forgiving love of their Author and Source. Having humbled himself in acknowledgment of this fact and having entered into covenants and

---

[49]Matthew 18:2; John 14:6.

ordinances incident to his allegiance, he has at least to some degree "put off the natural man" and become a creature capable of enjoying, appreciating, valuing, and loving profoundly.[50]

11. Earlier we noted (a) that genuine commitment to something higher than oneself means commitment to the will of another and (b) that it scarcely removes the tarnish of absurdity from one's strivings if this will is that of another mortal or mortals enthralled in the state of nature. But let the other will be the Lord's and this suspicion of absurdity vanishes. The reason is that there is no self-serving purpose in his act of proferring a stewardship to one of us. His intent is in fact to lend men power to direct their behavior in conformity with their ideals and thereby to give integrity, dignity, and significance to their lives. Indeed, he even designs to share a portion of this very role of his with us (our being willing) so that we can employ this power to assist in bringing about these same effects in others. The only self-transcendent purpose available to us is the one self-transcendent purpose that exists—His. We leave behind the absurdly head-

---

[50]Recalling his experiences with his university colleagues B. West Belnap (to whom this volume is dedicated) said just prior to his death: "[T]here were . . . times that we . . . talked together and even argued together. At the time it seemed so important that a certain point of view . . . be taken on a point of doctrine, and sometimes our discussions would become almost heated to the point that . . . there were occasions when I would go home not feeling really good inside, feeling that maybe the person with whom I had been discussing might not feel good about me. . . . As I've lain here, somehow the differences that we had, the little antagonisms that developed, seem so unimportant . . . . I've been thinking about some of these men. . . . Since I've been here, something has happened; some of these same men have turned out to be the men that have done so much for me. . . . I realize [now that] far more important than any doctrine that we ever discussed was the importance of love for each other. And I have come to love these brethren more than life itself. As I . . . think about all of the wonderful things that have been mine, . . . there has come into my heart an appreciation for the fact that the most important thing in life is the love that we have for each other. Today, more than ever before in my life, there has come into my heart [the realization that] the greatest thing that has come in my reflections has been to learn the love of Christ, and that all else relatively is unimportant."[50]

The point of view expressed in these words is one of the rarest achievements of the human mind and heart; few men succeed in staying true to principle without losing the capacity to love. That he was one of these made West Belnap one of the great godly men to have graced the earth. (Recounted by Ben E. Lewis at the funeral of B. West Belnap.)

strong and self-involved natural man that has taken unrighteous dominion in us when we commit ourselves to labor obediently in the Savior's work of helping others also to abandon that old and foolish man and join his cause. It is for these reasons that faith in and faithfulness to the Savior constitute the one mode in which true commitment can be made.

Nothing but a Being of infinite love could, as object of our unconditional commitment, make possible the integration of the personal and social aspects of our lives into unity of self, unity of marriage, unity of brotherhood in the priesthood, and unity with Him. This realization may help us appreciate the feeling behind something Dostoevsky wrote in a letter (he was sentenced to death at twenty-two for "revolutionary activities," had the sentence commuted at the last moment, and then spent four years in Siberia, on the march to which a peasant woman gave him a New Testament that he read constantly during his miserable detention): "If anyone could prove to me that Christ is outside the truth, and if the truth really did exclude Christ, I should prefer to stay with Christ and not with the truth."[51]

Sacrifice

We read in Hebrews that the Lord's untainted sacrifice of himself can make holy and untainted all who, though having been tainted, consecrate themselves in the pattern he set. All else besides fidelity to his Father's will became as dead to him—nothing could cause him to compromise his commitment (upon which depended his very meaning as men's Savior) to mere enticement. Short of this unwavering steadfastness, his flesh would not have "become subject even unto death."[52] His personal will would have undermined his commitment; it would not have been "swal-

---

[51]*Letters of Fyodor Dostoevsky*, trans. E. C. Mayne, p. 71, quoted in C. M. Woodhouse, *Dostoevsky* (London: Arthur Barker, 1951), p. 89.
[52]Mosiah 15:7.

lowed up in the will of the Father."[53] The forces of dissolu-
tion and death that entice us to yield to selfish desire and
thereby to compromise our integrity would not have been
outlasted and thereby overcome by him.

We too must be committed even to the point of death,
or else we shall never be whole. To say that we must be this
committed is to say that everything else must die for us
relative to him and the performance of his will. Only if we
are as strangers and foreigners on the earth, engaged in a
pilgrimage for a society not found as yet, a city whose foundation God has laid, will we hold out until the end. Of Abraham, Sarah, Isaac, and Jacob, Paul wrote:

> They were not yet in possession of the things promised, but had
> seen them far ahead and hailed them, and confessed themselves no more
> than strangers or passing travelers on earth. Those who use such language
> show plainly that they are looking for a country of their own. *If their
> hearts had been in the country they had left, they could have found
> opportunity to return.* Instead, we find them longing for a better country
> —I mean, the heavenly one. That is why God is not ashamed to be called
> their God.[54]

Short of this, a man can have no confidence that his
course in life is pleasing to God and that it flows from a
genuine commitment.

> [A] religion that does not require the sacrifice of all things never
> has power sufficient to produce the faith necessary unto life and salvation;
> . . . the faith necessary unto the enjoyment of life and salvation never
> could be obtained with the sacrifice of all earthly things. When a man has
> offered in sacrifice all that he has for the truth's sake, not even withhold-
> ing his life, and believing before God that he has been called to make this
> sacrifice because he seeks to do His will, he does know, most assuredly,
> that God does and will accept his sacrifice and offering.[55]

If (and only if) the objects and experiences native to
this world are not a man's treasure, but are instead willingly

[53]Ibid.
[54]Hebrews 11:13-16. Italics added.
[55]*Lectures on Faith*, 6:7.

surrendered whenever they are required of him by his Lord, they are, like Isaac under Abraham's knife, given back—they are for the first time profoundly enjoyed. Wrote C. S. Lewis:

> The essence of religion, in my view, is the thirst for an end higher than natural ends; the finite self's desire for, and acquiesence in, and self-rejection in favor of, an object wholly good and wholly good for it. That the self-rejection will turn out also to be a self-finding, that the bread cast upon the waters will be found after many days, that to die is to live—these are sacred paradoxes.[56]

In mortality, it seems, there is an inverse variation between satisfaction pursued and satisfaction obtained, for a capacity to enjoy cannot be separated from an unqualified willingness to sacrifice enjoyment in favor of what is right whenever the two conflict. To recur to our earlier metaphor, whoever preciously cherishes every bud and blossom because, as he thinks, they contain all of the promise he will ever possess of fruitfulness and happiness will, when the harvest comes, become suspicious and bitter about the enterprise called life. But whoever submits to being pruned and cropped according to a plan fully known only to his Lord will one day bear and enjoy fruit beyond belief.

> Except a corn of wheat fall into the ground and die, it abideth alone: but if it die, it bringeth forth much fruit.
> He that loveth his life shall lose it; and he that hateth his life in this world shall keep it unto life eternal.[57]

Faith and Reason

In the light of the thoughts in this essay, the propositions of the preceding paragraphs appear obviously true. At other times or to other people they may seem unreasonable, even nearly paradoxical. Like optical illusions, they seem now one thing, now another. This phenomenon is not difficult to explain.

---

[56]*A Mind Awake: An Anthology of C. S. Lewis*, ed. by Clyde S. Kilby (New York: Harcourt, Brace and World, 1969), p. 111.
[57]John 12:24-25 (King James version).

Whether the propositions are reasonable or unreasonable depends upon one's point of view. To the man whose own reason is the ultimate standard for appraising the worth of things, they seem foolish. But to the man who trusts his reason only secondarily and the object of his faith primarily, the propositions are the very soul of reasonableness. And it is the latter man who is right. For commitment to something higher than self, or faith, is more significant than anything reason can justify precisely, because, as we have seen, all of life, even—nay, especially—the activity of reason, is pointless and absurd without it. Faith is the ground of meaningful existence; in its absence no human enterprise can matter— including, I stress again, the enterprise of reasoning. Whether there is a point to being reasonable depends upon a person's faithfulness, but not the other way round. Faith is the fundament even of reason.[58]

From the natural man's viewpoint then, the notion of self-pruning that introduced this essay seems unreasonable, but only because his allegiances provide him with a hidden and false premise—the premise that reason is self-certifying —that enables him to think so. From the spiritual man's point of view, there is nothing more reasonable than this notion, for he rejects the false premise. For him, reason is certified by faith. Reason itself, when faithfully employed, can help us discover reason's dependency and convince ourselves how reasonable faith can be.

---

[58]This is why I think it is appropriate to speak of a "leap of faith," which outdistances any conclusions that can be reached by thinking alone.

The Meaning
of
Love

Reed H. Bradford

REED H. BRADFORD is professor of sociology at Brigham Young University. He has been recognized worldwide as an expert on family living. He holds master's degrees from Louisiana State University and Harvard, and a Ph.D. from Harvard. He has taught throughout the United States and in the Near East. His teaching success has been recognized by his selection as professor of the year and by his receiving the Karl G. Maeser Award for teaching excellence.

He has served the Church as a missionary to Germany, as a member of the Sunday School general board, and as the executive secretary for both the Adult Correlation Committee and the Youth and Young Adult Correlation Committee.

He and his wife, the former Shirley Aamodt, are the parents of seven children.

THE MEANING OF LOVE

Reed H. Bradford

Guidelines to Divine Meaning

"While such devices as computers and the communication satellite system are now able to provide the greatest amount of information in the shortest time ever available to men, the ordinary person actually knows less about what is really going on in the world than before these systems were evolved. He is inundated with facts, but provided with no *frame of reference* in which to assess them."[1] There is a way to find a solution to this problem, however. It lies in finding the fundamental principles that unify and give meaning to specific events and situations. These general principles become the guidelines for behavior. Elsewhere I have identified this concept as the "Hub of the Wheel."[2]

The Savior clearly explained the "Hub of the Wheel" of one's life:

> Then one of them, which was a lawyer, asked him a question, tempting him, and saying, Master, which is the great commandment in the law? Jesus said unto him, Thou shalt love the Lord thy God with all thy heart, and with all thy soul, and with all thy mind. This is the first and great commandment. And the second is like unto it, Thou shalt love thy neighbour as thyself. *On these two commandments hang all the law and the prophets.*[3]

To love the way our Heavenly Father, the Savior, and

---

[1] Editorial entitled "After Thought" in the *Deseret News*, December 25, 1971, p. A-12.
[2] See *A Teacher's Quest* (Provo, Utah: Brigham Young University Press, 1971), p. 4.
[3] Matthew 22:35-40. Italics added.

the Holy Ghost love is to give life its greatest and most edifying meaning. But what are the characteristics of that love?

Limited Loving

In order to understand a great principle in its clearest
form, it is helpful to see (1) some contrasts to it or (2) some
limited examples of it. The following cases illustrate the way
many people behave toward others.

He Smashed It Before My Eyes[4]

It is rather difficult for me to draw a line or designate explicitly
where normal citizenship behavior ends and juvenile delinquency begins.
Long before I began to commit crimes against society, I was fully
aware of my intense feelings of hostility and disregard for the legal
code and moral restrictions of our society. . . .

My childhood years were ones of great anxiety in which I had
feelings of discontent whenever I was at home. The display of love was
almost non-existent between my father and me, for many times I had
experienced traumatic situations at his hands. The first instance of re-
membrance occurred when I was only five years of age. After finding a
sack full of baby kittens near a river, I gave all but one away, keeping a
small crippled one for myself. A few months later, after I had nursed it
to a point of complete recovery, my father informed me that we were
moving and the kitten had to be put away. He proceeded to place the
kitten on a boulder, and picking up a large rock, he hurled it at the
kitten, smashing it before my eyes. In this instance, as in others that
followed, I ran off and hid myself, cursing my father and vowing one
day to pay him back.

This opportunity presented itself when at the age of fourteen we
moved to a large city, where I immediately became acquainted with the
hoodlums of my junior high school. Within a relatively short time, I
accepted an invitation to join one of the most intricately operated gangs
I've ever seen. This idea appealed to me immensely, as I now felt wanted
and accepted; whereas at home I had never received any overt acts of
love from my father, and my mother was a passive, easy-going person,
never cognizant of my intense feelings. [This gang became the center and
focus of this girl's life. She took part in different types of crime such as
smuggling, dope peddling, shoplifting, burglary, and adultery.]

Many of us had to lead two entirely different lives—one at home

---

[4]An anonymous but true incident.

associating with our families, and one as a member of a secret society. Most of us were deliberately doing things we knew our families wouldn't approve. We wanted to hurt them in any way we could, since we all felt we had been inadequately treated at home. . . .

Soon I was working in dope traffic in a very intense way and I became interested in one of the pushers. Our relationship deepened and he began to come to my house to take me out on dates. My father disliked him intensely. This pleased me and I delighted in our relationship merely for this reason. Being one of the top pushers, he had been instructed never to use dope himself. However, one day after we had made the round, we decided to try a "bennie" (benzedrine). This was my start on "junk." In the next few weeks, I attended a number of "tea parties" (marijuana) and found this to be a greater kick than bennies. It wasn't long till I found myself taking dope out of our supplies. Eventually I was found out and ostracized from the gang.

But I had to keep my habit fed. A contact in a doctor's office helped me out a little, but she could take only a little codeine or morphine, and I began to want more.

To sustain my expensive habit, I began to "freelance" and located a number of other "hop-heads" interested in getting money to buy drugs. We committed several burglaries and obtained some money but it was never enough. . . .

At this period of my life my parents decided to move to another town in another part of the state. When I started high school in this new community, I was hooked miserably by the "hypo." I began to hate everyone and everything. Life was no longer important, and twice I attempted suicide, but I was discovered by my friends and saved in time. Consequently, I decided that I would just die slowly by increasing overdoses of heroin."

Steve, Go Wash Your Hands[5]

My silent prayers in school increased in frequency and intensity when Steve entered my third grade class.

Steve had the roundest eyes, dirtiest hands, and wildest imagination I've ever known. These three characteristics worked together toward the disruption of my class's decorum and severely tried my professional patience.

Why couldn't he be quiet and clean some mornings? Why couldn't he at least have clean hands? Why must so many mornings have messy beginnings? End-of-the-day filth was bad enough but more easily for-

[5]Jeanne H. Ward, "Today's Education," *Journal of the National Education Association*, December, 1970, pp. 42-43. Used by permission.

given. Trouble every morning? That was just too much. Indoor dirt, mud and snow in season, food, ink from a detonated ballpoint pen, nail polish, glue, malodorous traces of this and that from barn or field— these and more made Steve a frequent visitor to the washbowls in the boys' lavatory. The fact that his goings and comings to the washroom cut into his class and study time considerably gave him not an instant of regret.

Spring was Steve's best season. The reawakening of the earth was an inspiration to him.

One spring morning Steve's always loud voice started the school day with:

"This is a real tick with blood in him. He told me his name is Harold. . . ."

(Be patient. Maybe this boy has problems you know nothing of.)

"Steve, throw Harold away and go wash your hands!" Then a little later:

"This bird flew down and asked me to hold it for a while, but it left some little white bugs."

(He must have no one to show things to at home. Act interested!)

"Steve, get rid of all the white bugs. Go wash your hands!"

And again:

"Mr. Craig's dog asked me to help him get a gopher. I did. The gopher cried."

(Why don't his parents discuss the gopher, clean Steve up, and then send him to school?)

"Steve, go wash your hands."

Frustrated and annoyed, I put Steve's name on the list of the school's home visitor. She reported back that there was trouble between the parents but that the home had acceptable standards and there didn't seem to be an obvious reason why Steve shouldn't come to school clean. Steve's mother (who looked chronically worried, the visitor said) insisted that Steve's hands were clean when he left the house but that he had always been inquisitive about animals and things and couldn't resist handling whatever aroused his curiosity.

Soon again at the beginning of the school day:

"This fish in the crick came up three times. The first time he said, 'Steve, make a wish'. . . ."

(Can't you listen and see how the story comes out? Try!) . . .

"Look, those smooth rocks are magic. If you rub them and say, 'rocka-wocka rocka-wocka,' they will make something nice happen."

(Why don't you listen? Why don't *you* make something nice happen? Why don't *you* make something nice happen?) [But busy with other things, she didn't listen and didn't make something nice happen to him.]

Sometimes it wasn't nature, just the cafeteria that caused a problem: "Peanut butter is really glue. I made this myself from my own peanuts. Look at these papers stick together."

(It *is* remarkably adhesive, you know.) . . .

Days later, I asked for a second home visit. The visitor reported that there was real strife between the parents, but Steve's mother promised that his hands would be cleaner when he came to school.

The next morning:

"A robin gave me one of her eggs, but it's smashed. There was a baby bird in it. I'm sorry."

(When you were young, didn't you ever touch a robin's egg?) . . .

The next day:

"Our cat had seven kittens last night. I watched and helped, but she screamed anyway."

(Oh, no!)

"Steve, go wash your hands!"

Desperate, I decided to make a visit to Steve's home myself. As I stepped onto the small porch, I heard a woman's terrified voice saying, "No, you can't. Put it down! At least think of Steve."

"OK, but just once more and you get it!"

I ran away quietly, but my heart pounded for an hour afterward.

The next morning Steve was not in an announcing mood. He said not a word for almost an hour. Then he crept up to my desk and whispered, "My daddy shot my mother in the chest last night and then he shot himself. I touched my mother."

"Oh Steve! Oh, Stevie! Oh, Stevie, come here."

The Face[6]

I saw him on the street only this morning.

Already late for work, I cut through Skid Row to catch my 8:32 commuter. It was a miserable morning, the sky a musky gray made of factory smoke and soot and dirty rain. Even my new coat with its fashionable big collar turned up against my face could not hide the dingy alleys covered with broken glass. Scrawny cats pawed through the garbage cans that lined the narrow passageways between the bars. I saw the names above the doors—the Blue-tailed Fly, the Painted Lady, Janie's.

I berated myself for having tried to save time by the short cut. Lowering my head deeper into my collar, I hurried around the corner, running full tilt into a weaving, lurching man. He fell heavily to the sidewalk in front of me. I stared with horrified fascination at him. His

---

[6]Written by one of my students. Used by permission.

clothes were filthy and he reeked of garlic and liquor. His unshaven face was clean only where the rain ran down it in tiny streams. His uncombed hair was as black as the eyes that stared dully at me, devoid of any expression. For a second that stretched into an eon, I stood there frozen. Then, as he softly called my name, I turned and ran and ran until I saw the familiar station, the people I knew, and the sights and sounds of sanity. But the soft call of my name still sounded in my ears.

Sinking exhausted into my train chair, I closed my eyes to shut out what I had seen. The derelict on Skid Row was not unknown to me. It was the face of Jim, a boy I had known years ago in grammar and high school in the small community in which we had both been reared.

It was a gossipy little town, closely knit by a common religion and by the stand-off attitude shown those who violated any of its codes. Jim's mother was an alcoholic, and the neighbors could hear his father and mother quarreling long into the night. As this news reached the ears of the townspeople, more and more of Jim's playmates were forbidden to associate with him. My folks were more lenient, and as the years went by, he came often to our home.

But when his father committed suicide while Jim was still in high school, the last of his friends drifted away, and he became more lonely and more resentful of society. To fight back at the rules that had excluded him from other groups, he began to cut school, and the hoods he associated with were no strangers to police records. Finally, just like all the rest, I turned my back on him too.

By leaving him now in the alley, I was turning my back on him again. Our town gave him a start toward Skid Row, but I was pushing him the last mile by taking away his last hope of acceptance. As I thought about him, I remembered the lines of a poem he once read to me:

> You regret
> That memory is a tiny cup
> So soon over-brimming.
>
> Ah,
> Would that the tiny cup
> Were deeply cracked,
> Retaining nothing.
> —Paul Eldrigde, "Two Opinions"

In the kind of relationships depicted in the case studies above there are some distinctive characteristics.

1. The individual tends to be egocentric in the sense that he may be very sensitive to his own desires but insensitive

to the desires and feelings of others. (The father thought only of the inconvenience of taking the kitten with them. He never once thought what it symbolized to his daughter.)

2. When another person does not behave the way one wants him to behave, one becomes irritated with his behavior and does all kinds of things to try "to get even." He punishes him. (The girl in the first case study went out and did all kinds of things she knew would cause her father pain, because of the inconsiderate way he had treated her.)

3. One pays a terrible price for trying "to get even." (The girl engaged in activities that did not produce a positive development of her personality. They enslaved her. Also, her contributions to the lives of others were largely negative. They produced resentment, perhaps hatred, withdrawal, and unnecessary sorrow.)

4. Some individuals often have the right inclinations and motives. (The teacher would think of Steve's behavior and sense and feel that she ought to help him. But she did not act on those inclinations. She let minor things become of greater significance than major ones. Is there anything more important than a divine, human soul and its legitimate needs?)

5. One is not really concerned about another human soul. When one relates to others, he thinks in terms of what the "others" are going to do for him. (In most cases, politicians kiss babies not because they are primarily interested in the babies, but because they hope their parents will vote for them.)

In this system of behaving, if one does a favor for another person, he expects the other person will do something in return for him. "A person who fails to reciprocate favors is accused of ingratitude. This very accusation indicates that reciprocation is expected."[7] The failure to reciprocate means that something negative will occur in the relationship. It

---

[7]Peter M. Blau, *Exchange and Power in Social Life* (New York: John Wiley and Sons, 1964), p. 16.

might consist in the adoption of such behaviors as pouting, insulting, withdrawal, or rejection.

(It was tragic that the only people in the town who took any real interest in Jim were found in *one* home and even they began to become indifferent to him.)

6. Some individuals define love as a limited kind of "harmony" with another person. A boy says to a girl he is dating, "I love you," and what he actually means is that he is emotionally and sexually attracted to her. Later on if he marries her, and this attraction is the chief basis for the marriage, he and she may end up having all kinds of conflict and problems and divorce each other. They were married physically for a time, but hardly in any other way.

Such is the conditional and limited nature of these definitions of love.

A Divine Definition of Love

Let us now turn to a definition of love that involves the most edifying, fulfilling, and actualizing potentials for a divine human soul.

Let us begin by asking, "What is the final intended destiny of man as seen by his Creator, our Heavenly Father?" In many different places in the scriptures the Lord defined that destiny. For example, he said: "I am Jesus Christ, the Son of God, who was crucified for the sins of the world, even as many as will believe on my name, that they may become the sons of God, even one in me as I am one in the Father, as the Father is one in me, that we may be one."[8] Certainly one might also say for a woman that she might "become" his daughter. John expressed the same thought when he said: "Beloved, now are we the sons of God, and it doth not yet appear what we shall be: but we know that, when he shall appear, we shall be like him."[9]

What does it mean to "become" his son or his daughter?

---

[8]Doctrine and Covenants 35:2.
[9]1 John 3:2.

Are we not already his sons and daughters? Indeed we are. He organized the intelligences and gave them a spirit form.[10] Each of us has had a long experience before we came here to live upon this earth. To "become" the son or daughter of our Heavenly Father means to incorporate in our personalities the same qualities and characteristics, the same principles and the same behavior patterns, that have made him the great, wise, powerful (righteously powerful), loving, and fulfilled person that he is.

Let us analyze some of those qualities and principles as seen in the Savior, the person who exemplifies them better than any individual who has lived upon the earth.

The Savior as Our Model

The Savior said that whosoever had seen him had also seen our Heavenly Father, so that seeing what kind of person he is, he can also understand the kind of being our Heavenly Father is.

He Develops His Own Potentials

"And Jesus increased in wisdom and stature. . . ."[11] "And I, John, saw that he received not of the fulness at first, but received grace for grace."[12] He constantly admonished each of us to do the same. "Verily I say men should be anxiously engaged in a good cause, and do many things of their own free will, and bring to pass much righteousness. For the power is in them, wherein they are agents unto themselves."[13] Our Heavenly Father, the Savior, the Holy Ghost, and many other individuals can be of great assistance to us in our quest to become his sons or daughters, but we *ourselves* must expend the effort to acquire knowledge, wisdom, skills of various kinds, and the capacity to "overcome all things" that would deter us from that final goal.

----

[10]See Abraham 3:22-36.
[11]Luke 2:52.
[12]Doctrine and Covenants 93:12-13.
[13]Doctrine and Covenants 58:27-28.

In this world many individuals become discouraged because they compare themselves with others and conclude that these "others" are superior to them. It is true that another person may have some gift that I do not possess, or perhaps he possesses it to a greater degree than I do. Nevertheless, I must remember that each of us is a child of a divine Creator. That fact alone means that I have invested in me some of his potentials. Elder Hugh B. Brown is credited with having expressed the thought that "he who says he is inferior is criticizing his Creator in a negative way."

I have found several things to be helpful in discovering and developing one's gifts.

1. Obtaining knowledge about myself. W. I. Thomas said that "if men define situations as real, they are real in their consequences."[14] Once I accepted the fact that I am a son of my Heavenly Father, I began to comprehend something about my particular potentials. I took tests of various kinds prepared by competent people who had deep insights about human behavior. I did not take them too seriously in the sense that I thought they had final answers as to what I am, but I did find some of them useful in indicating *some* of my characteristics.

I asked several individuals who had had a close association with me for a long time to try to give me an objective analysis of myself—what they considered my gifts and limitations to be. This proved to be very helpful, since we often do not see ourselves as others see us. They pointed out things to me that I had never considered before.

When I was young, I began a practice I learned from the Savior. He often went "by himself" to commune with our Heavenly Father, to think about the goals he was pursuing, to consider the methods of achieving his goals, and other profoundly important and meaningful things. I refer to this as "the art of evaluation." When one is by himself, he is free from the normal activities of life that may be dis-

---

[14]See Lewis A. Coser and Bernard Rosenberg, *Sociological Theory* (New York: Collier-Macmillan Company, 1964), p. 232.

tracting. As Carlyle said: "Silence is the element in which great things fashion themselves."

2. Understanding and implementing his principles takes time. There are various levels of understanding. I have some comprehension of a principle when I *memorize* it. I have gone beyond this level if I can *explain* it to someone else. I have reached a still deeper level if I identify with it and have a *feeling* about it. If I receive a spiritual confirmation concerning it through the gift of the Holy Ghost, my understanding is much more profound. Finally if I put it into practice, I am at the depth level of understanding. As the Savior said: "If any man will *do* his will, he shall *know* of the doctrine, whether it be of God, or whether I speak of myself."[15] As one reverent and devoted follower of the Lord said, "I not only obey the Lord, I also agree with him." Of course there are also other things that he and we would agree that we do because we have faith and trust in him, even though we do not fully understand his teachings.

Some of his disciples had been with him for three years and, in spite of all the glorified experiences they had had with him, they did as he predicted: "All ye shall be offended because of me this night."[16] In his hour of greatest suffering preceding his crucifixion, "all the disciples forsook him and fled."[17] Later, however, when they had arrived at a new understanding of him they stood by him; they were loyal to him in the deepest sense. When Peter and some of the other apostles were threatened with death for having taught his principles, Peter, answering for them all, said, "We ought to obey God rather than men."[18] After they had been beaten and warned that they should not speak in his name again, "they departed . . . rejoicing that they were counted worthy to suffer shame for his name. And daily in the temple, and in every house, they ceased not to teach . . . Jesus Christ."[19]

------
[15]John, 7:17.
[16]Matthew 26:31.
[17]Matthew 26:56.
[18]Acts 5:29.
[19]Acts 5:41-42.

I have found it useful to take one of his principles at a
time and think about it, read what he said about it and how
he implemented it, study what others have said and done in
relation to it, and then seek for an evaluation from my Heavenly Father of my understanding of the principle. "You must
study it out in your mind; then you must ask me if it be
right, and if it is right I will cause that your bosom shall
burn within you; therefore, you shall feel that it is right."[20]
Of course one must learn to distinguish between emotional
desires and divine affirmation.

Thus growth is a gradual process. He gives unto "the
faithful line upon line, precept upon precept."[21] If a person
possesses this kind of righteous motivation and extends this
kind of devotion, he can be assured of the Lord's forgiveness
for his sins. "Behold, he who has repented of his sins, the
same is forgiven, and I, the Lord, remember them no more."[22]
In spite of his denial of the Savior three times in one night,
Peter later demonstrated great devotion to him and his principles. Alma, though he committed many grievous sins for
many years of his life, subsequently, through a personal commitment to him, assisted thousands "to taste of the exceeding
joy of which I did taste; that they might also be born of God,
and be filled with the Holy Ghost."[23]

He Demonstrates Maturity in Major Areas of Personality

One might mention five aspects of personality in which
this maturity is manifest.

1. Intellectual. Each of us has the ability to think, to
reason without prejudice. If one's motive is to find the truth,
he does not hold to a given idea simply because he himself
has held it. If he does hold to it, in spite of reliable evidence
to the contrary, he is defending not the truth, but his ego.
The Lord said: "And even so I have sent mine everlasting

[20]Doctrine and Covenants 9:8.
[21]Doctrine and Covenants 98:12.
[22]Doctrine and Covenants 58:42.
[23]Alma 36:24.

covenant into the world, to be a light to the world. . . . Wherefore, come ye unto it, and with him that cometh I will reason as with men in days of old, and I will show unto you my strong reasoning."[24] Does he not expect us, when we have important decisions to make, to think soundly, obtain the best information available, benefit from our experience, and seek his inspiration and confirmation before finally acting?

2. Emotional. The emotions, which are part of our personality, are not in and of themselves evil. The key issue is *how* we express them. "To every thing there is a season, and a time to every purpose under the heaven: A time to be born, and a time to die; . . . a time to weep, and a time to laugh."[25] Our task is to learn to *manage* the emotions and not to permit them to manage us. Through the use of intelligence and the gift of the Holy Ghost, such an ability can be greatly enhanced. I have found it useful to think in terms of "the diamond and the glass imitation of the diamond." Some satisfactions, though momentarily exciting, end up by enslaving the individual. Others continually give fulfillment and joy.

3. Physical. He said, "the spirit and the body are the soul of man."[26] The body is the temple of the spirit, and I should therefore eat a proper diet, exercise regularly, obtain the proper amount of rest, and have an edifying attitude about life, because the mind and the spirit affect the functioning of the body and vice versa.

4. Social. He is able to work effectively with others. If we follow his example, we develop our own potentials and then freely share them with others. Thus there is a constant enrichment for everyone. Being sensitive to the ultimate goal of "becoming like him" makes such a process easier. One "keeps in mind the end from the beginning."

------

[24]Doctrine and Covenants 45:9-10.
[25]Ecclesiastes 3:1, 2, 4.
[26]Doctrine and Covenants 88:15.

5. Spiritual. He knows that "there is a law irrevocably decreed in heaven before the foundations of this world upon which all blessings are predicated. And when we obtain any blessing from God, it is by obedience to the law upon which it is predicated."[27] If one patiently tries to reach the depth levels of understanding of His basic spiritual principles, he gradually becomes more like Him.

He Has a Personal Concern for Each Human Soul

Individuals who have an inadequate understanding of the Lord's definition of love do not perceive the magnificent opportunity of having the same sensitive concern for every person that one has for himself. Perhaps the following diagram might be helpful in understanding that opportunity.

---

[27]Doctrine and Covenants 130:20-21.

My Network of Relationships

If I develop my own gifts and then freely share them with anyone who desires to share them, and they do the same for me, then *together* we are greater and more fulfilled than we could ever be alone. This is why the lines of the diagram are broken. It means that there is a "mutual enrichment" occurring among us all.

Thus one could say that though there are *many* members of the family, there is only *one* family. This is why the Savior requested that we address each other as "brother" or "sister." Because that is exactly what we are, brothers and sisters who are children of the same Father. Paul understood this so well.

Now there are diversities of gifts, but the same Spirit. And there are differences of administrations, but the same Lord. . . . But the manifestation of the Spirit is given to every man to profit withal. . . . For as the body is one, and hath many members, and all the members of that one body, being many, are one body: so also is Christ. For by one Spirit are we all baptized into one body, whether we be Jews or Gentiles, whether we be bond or free; and have been all made to drink into one Spirit. . . . If the ear shall say, because I am not the eye, I am not the body; is it therefore not of the body? If the whole body were an eye, where were the hearing? . . . [But] the eye cannot say unto the hand, I have no need of thee: nor again the head to the feet, I have no need of you. . . . There should be no schism in the body; but that the members should have the same care one for another. And whether one member suffer, all the members suffer with it; or one member be honoured, all the members rejoice with it. Now ye are the body of Christ, and members in particular.[28]

Or as John Donne expressed it: "No man is an island entire of itself: every man is a piece of the continent, a part of the main. If a clod be washed away by the sea, Europe is the less. . . . Any man's death diminishes me, because I am involved in mankind, and therefore never send to know for whom the bell tolls; it tolls for thee."[29]

---

[28]1 Corinthians 12:4, 5, 7, 12, 21, 25-27.
[29]John Donne, *Meditation* 17.

The Divine Dialogue

In helping me to love the way the Savior loves, I found it useful to give the name "the Divine Dialogue" to the method of interaction such a love involves. It has the following characteristics:

1. The individuals involved in the interaction or communication always seek the truth. Only the truth permits us to reach the final fulfillment. Building one's life on error or deception is like building a house on sand.

2. Each person is sensitive to every other in the sense the previous discussion has indicated. Three things I have found help me to manifest that sensitivity:

a. The sensitive line. One who loves the way He loves would not consciously hurt the feelings of another person. He would seek to build the relationship in a positive way. Generally, one "crosses the sensitive line" in his relationship with others by the infliction of physical pain, sarcasm, pouting, using humor to embarrass someone, or by not creatively listening to them. One of my friends stated that his father usually cut him off in the middle of a sentence and never let him really express his thoughts.

If one does cross the sensitive line, he should apologize. If such an apology is done with the right intent and motivation, it tends to restore the relationship.

b. Empathy. Empathy means that one tries consciously to see a situation or circumstance from the point of view of another person. I find it useful when I see one of my children doing something that I consider to be immature to ask myself the question: "How did things seem to you when you were that age?" This permits me to gain new and meaningful insights and makes my subsequent behavior more positive and mature.

c. The final goal of fulfillment. In a way, the goal of fulfillment colors everything I do, because I ask myself the question, "Will what I am about to do help this person to reach his final intended destiny or will it be likely to deter him from it?"

3. We should strive to reach an agreement. True, each of us is unique in some ways. Each of us has had a different experience in a number of instances, and each of us has different knowledge and wisdom. Nevertheless He has expressed the idea that we should be "one." This means that we should be one in the main goals we pursue, the method of achieving those goals, and the spirit that characterizes our relationships. Two things will help us achieve it. First, one must study His principles and seek to live them. Secondly, one must try to be worthy to receive His inspiration. Think of the implications of His statement: "And every decision made by either of these quorums must be by the unanimous voice of the same."[30]

4. One must keep in mind the "big picture." The "big picture" has two fundamental aspects. In the first place I must think, "How will my behavior affect me—not just for the next few minutes, hours, or weeks, but for the rest of eternity?" As a girl once expressed it, "I wish I had known five minutes before I committed adultery how I would feel five minutes after I gave my child away." Secondly, I must remember that my action will affect not only me but every life I touch, either directly or indirectly.

5. The spirit of the relationship is positive and edifying. This kind of loving can only be experienced in its deepest and most divine form when one has "been born again" and received the influence of the Holy Ghost. What kind of influence is it? "Remember faith, virtue, knowledge, temperance, patience, brotherly kindness, godliness, charity, humility, diligence."[31] "Charity suffereth long, and is kind, charity envieth not; charity vaunteth not itself, is not puffed up. Doth not behave itself unseemly, . . . is not easily pro-

---

[30]Doctrine and Covenants 107:27.
[31]Doctrine and Covenants 4:6.

voked, thinketh no evil. Rejoiceth not in iniquity, but rejoiceth in the truth."[32]

When one sees another person make a mistake, one's first
thought is not to get even with him, but to help him. "Wherefore, I say unto you, that ye ought to forgive one another;
for he that forgiveth not his brother his trespasses standeth
condemned before the Lord; for there remaineth in him the
greater sin."[33] One may feel sorrow over the misbehavior of
another person, but he never resents him as a person.

Thus love as defined by the Savior means fulfillment.
It also means joy. He indicated that everything that he had
done while upon the earth was designed to achieve such an
end. Shortly after his crucifixion he said, "These things have
I spoken unto you, that my joy might remain in you, and
that your joy might be full."[34]

There are many examples that might be given of this
kind of loving. Space will permit only one.

Johnny Lingo

Patricia McGeer tells of a yong teenage girl named Sarita
whom everyone, including her parents, thought of as being
inferior. Her father was afraid that no man would ever
request her to be his bride. Then one day an intelligent and
sensitive man known to be "the sharpest trader" in that part
of the South Seas came into the village where Sarita lived.

When a man wanted a wife, it was the custom to give
her father a certain number of cows for permission to marry
her. For some reason that no one could comprehend, Johnny
Lingo asked for Sarita. "Maybe when it comes to love, he's
either blind or stupid," they concluded. They expected, however, that he would offer no more than one or, at the most,
two cows for her.

But when Johnny Lingo came to her home, he went
straight up to her father, Sam Karoo, grasped his hand, and

---

[32]1 Corinthians 13:4-6.
[33]Doctrine and Covenants 64:9.
[34]John 15:11.

said, "Father of Sarita, I offer eight cows for your daughter." And he delivered the cows. Everyone was dumbfounded.

Johnny took his bride to the island of Choo. Patricia McGerr went to the island to try and unfathom the mystery of his marrying Sarita. When she met the slim, serious, and sensitive man, he welcomed her to his home with a grace that made her feel the owner. She was glad that from his own people he had respect unmingled with mockery. She told him that she had heard about him at Kinawata (where Sarita had been reared) and how they considered him to be a sharp trader. Then she indicated her curiosity as to why he had paid more for Sarita than had ever been paid for a wife in the whole history of the village.

"Always and forever," he said, "when they speak of marriage settlements, it will be remembered that Johnny Lingo paid eight cows for Sarita."

"So that's the answer," [Patricia McGreer continues] I thought with disappointment. All this mystery and wonder and the explanation is only vanity. It's not enough for his ego to be known as the smartest, the strongest, the quickest. He had to make himself famous for his way of buying a wife. I was tempted to deflate him by reporting that in Kiniwata he was laughed at for being a fool.

And then I saw her. Through the glass-beaded portieres that shimmered in the archway, I watched her enter the adjoining room to place a bowl of blossoms on the dining table. . . . She was [one] of the most beautiful women I have ever seen. . . . [She] had an ethereal loveliness that was at the same time from the heart of nature. . . .

When she was out of sight I turned back to Johnny Lingo and found him looking at me with eyes that reflected a deep pride in the girl.

"You admire her?" he murmured.

"She—she's glorious. Who is she?"

"My wife."

I stared at him blankly. . . . Before I could form a question he spoke again.

"That is Sarita."

"But she's not the Sarita from Kiniwata," I said.

"There is only one Sarita. . . . Perhaps you wish to say she does not look the way they say she looked in Kiniwata. . . . She doesn't. . . . Much in particular happened the day she went away."

"You mean she married you?"

"That yes. But most of all, I mean the arrangements for the marriage."

"Arrangements?"

"Do you ever think," he asked reflectively, "what it must mean to a woman to know that her husband-to-be has met with her father to settle the lowest price for which she can be bought? And then later, when all the women talk, . . . they boast of what their husbands paid for them. One says four cows, another maybe six. How does she feel, the woman who was sold for one or two? This could not happen to my Sarita."

"Then you paid that unprecedented number of cows just to make your wife happy?"

"Happy?" He seemed to turn the word over [in his soul]. "I wanted Sarita to be happy, . . . but I wanted more than that. You say she's different from the way they remember her in Kiniwata. This is true. Many things can change a woman. Things that happen inside, things that happen outside. But the thing that matters most is what she thinks about herself. In Kiniwata, Sarita believed she was worth nothing. Now she knows she is worth [very much]."

"Then you wanted—"

"I wanted to marry Sarita. I love her. . . ."

"But—" I was close to understanding.

"But," he finished softly, "I wanted [Sarita to become and eight-cow woman]."[35]

Three great blessings come from this kind of loving.

1. Here was a person everyone thought was inferior. It is sad that she could not have known that as a child of our Heavenly Father she had great potentials. But then one person, Johnny Lingo, saw in her the great possibilities of her life. And he backed his words with his deeds. This helped her to achieve a "breakthrough," and she became the magnificent person Johnny Lingo always knew she could become.

2. In the beginning of the relationship with Johnny Lingo, it was he who gave so much to her. He gave of his understanding, his patience, his knowledge, and of his continuing concern. But later she gave just as much to him. She gave her unique gifts as a woman and as a person.

---

[35]Patricia McGeer, "Johnny Lingo," *Woman's Day*, November 1965. Reprinted by permission of *Woman's Day*.

Now they were mutually enriching one another. Together they formed a "paired unity" in which they were free to develop their own gifts and abilities. But they were "one" in the main goals they pursued, the principles they used as guidelines for their behavior, and the spirit that characterized their relationship.

3. In the film entitled "Johnny Lingo," there is a scene in which Johnny gives Sarita a mirror as a symbol of his love for her. As he does so, she says to him, "Oh, I wish I had a gift for you." She was speaking from the depths of her soul. She was thinking of all the things her husband had done for her. It was spontaneous.

But just as spontaneously he said back to her, "Your gift for me can be seen by all who look at you." She was a magnificent woman, and he had played a key role in her achievement.

This kind of love provides the greatest motivation for each individual to reach the fulfillment and joy that our Heavenly Father always intended should be ours.

To the Youth of Zion

Neal A. Maxwell

NEAL A. MAXWELL is commissioner of education for the Church, a position he has held since August 1970. Prior to this appointment he was executive vice-president of the University of Utah. Since 1956 he has held several administrative positions at the university and prior to that he was legislative assistant to United States Senator Wallace F. Bennett.

He holds bachelor's and master's degrees from the University of Utah, and is the recipient of two honorary doctor's degrees. He has held many responsible civic and business positions, and presently is chairman of the Constitutional Revision Commission for the State of Utah.

In the Church he is a regional representative of the Twelve, and has been a bishop and a member of the Adult Correlation Committee and the YMMIA general board.

He is married to the former Colleen Hinckley, and they are the parents of four children.

TO THE YOUTH OF ZION

Neal A. Maxwell

One cannot have the experiences I have had in the past year without sensing how rapidly the Church is being internationalized. In recent months I have been in over twenty countries all over the world. It has been the kind of experience that has permitted me to see a good many of the one-quarter million students of the Church Education System, which includes fifty thousand institute students worldwide.

Because of that experience, I have had reinforced for me whose Church this really is and who manages and directs its affairs, in spite of the foibles and shortcomings of each of us. It has been a sobering year, a delightful year, and one reason that it has been delightful is that I have come back not only knowing afresh whose Church it is, but extremely impressed with our young Latter-day Saints the world over.

Down at the Church College of New Zealand the Maoris comprise two-thirds of the student body. They were in a national water polo championship tournament and refused to play on a Sunday, which necessitated their playing four matches on a Saturday, a very difficult task in that vigorous sport. But they did and won them all, and the tournament was over two days early.

One can go to Scotland and meet the Scottish Saints, to Germany, to Brazil, and to Tonga—it does not really matter where. The younger generation has been ushered onto the stage at a very fortuitous time for the Church, and I am deeply impressed with their courage and idealism.

Because I love them and am so impressed with the rich quality of our youth, may I share some observations with them that may be helpful in their everyday lives. The rest of this essay is addressed especially to the youth of the Church, but also to all youth everywhere, however old.

I believe that the Church is organized love as well as ordinances. I see it as administering affection as well as administering authority, and without this organized love, without this administered affection, the Church would not be able to provide all the support and strength that we need. If each of us were simply isolated Christians left with our own random impulses to do good, we simply would not be any match for the powers that are in the world, and we would fall "an unpitied sacrifice in the struggle." You are at an age where occasionally the institution of the Church may chafe a bit. But let us keep in mind that it is precisely because it *is* also organized love and administered affection —as well as ordinances and authority—that we are able to succeed where others fail.

Next, life is not any sandpile that we go to fresh each day to start from scratch. We inherit yesterday; time cannot be recycled! In terms of the speed with which time moves, it will close in on you very fast and you will be set with your habits and lifestyle locked in place pretty rigidly in the next couple of years—these things are alterable, to be sure, but it should be a source of great concern to each of us to do as much as we can while we are maximally plastic in terms of our personality and character and style. These observations are offered upon the assumption that you care about improvements in yourself that are appropriate for people in the Church who believe in a future in which we shall be together a million years from now.

It is important to understand that obedience is not simply a requirement of a capricious god who wants us to jump hurdles for him for the entertainment of the royal court. It is really the pleading of a loving Father to you and me to discover as quickly as we can what we will discover eventually—that there are key concepts and principles that make for happy survival in a planned but otherwise cold universe.

Faith and obedience compensate for the shortfall that is true of each of us in terms of our limited experience and limited knowledge. We simply have to rely on these other things to carry us forward at times, because our experience and our knowledge do fall short. And that pleading from a loving Father and his prophets here is to spare us the kind of pain that we will feel if we will not listen.

Second, your generation is rightfully concerned about ecology and the care of our "Eden" in terms of this planet earth. That is very appropriate. We *ought* to be concerned about the environment we transmit to our successors. But we really cannot have the full spirit of stewardship unless we are also concerned with the stewardship of self—because we transmit ourselves too. We are a part of the total environment that others experience, and if we are not "put together" spiritually, this can be just as devastating, and more so over the long haul, than for us to fail to transmit our environment in good shape and intact. The sewage of sin is so devastating downstream in life that it overshadows the physical effluence about which we have a right to be concerned. It is good that we care about what goes on in some of the things that are detrimental to our environment and to act wisely on those concerns, but where we differ from the world is that we have these concerns and others too.

I do not believe that there is any way to measure the rippling consequences, the tragic consequences, of an unloved, insufficiently disciplined Lee Harvey Oswald. If we are really concerned about human misery and pain, we have to be concerned with its real sources and not just with the symptoms that manifest themselves in a host of ways. What Lee Harvey Oswald did, what others have done because of the spiritual shortfall in their own lives and environments, will give us consequences with which we will live a lot longer than some of the other things about which we are visibly concerned.

Third, tomorrow always exists prenatally in today, which

carries the fetus of tomorrow. It is almost irrevocably shaped, and this is true of us as nations, as individuals, and as a Church. We cannot really care about the future in a complete way if we are insensitive to those dimensions of the present that will produce a tomorrow about which we would be deeply concerned if we only knew.

The insensitivity of the people of the time of Noah, if we had all the sociological and political data, would give us some interesting insights and parallels to our own time. The insensitivity then was gross and widespread and probably lasted until it began to rain and kept raining, by which time it was too late. In the same sense, when the Church expresses the concerns it does through its prophets and through you, hopefully, it is trying to guard against being encrusted with the kind of insensitivity that leads to widespread tragedy.

I am impressed with the sincerity of the prescriptions the world offers for some of the solutions that beset mankind. But the problem with the world's approach is that it often fails to diagnose the problem and therefore to provide any real and lasting cure. It is one thing to wring one's hands, but the wringing of hands, though it connotes anguish and even sincerity, is not the same thing as competency. Being concerned does not necessarily produce insights, and the insights necessary to the diagnosis of human ills are, in my judgment, contained in the gospel of Jesus Christ. What some of your associates and mine prescribe ironically would constitute giving mankind an aspirin when what we need is surgery.

What the world often prescribes stops short of real reform simply because men do not examine the root causes of human misery. I do not believe, for instance, that one can talk about prison reform in the wake of Attica and not raise searching questions about the relative quality of home life that those men had prior to their being incarcerated. If we are really concerned about human misery, we have to have prison reform, but we must have prior concern with causal factors in the institution of the family—and that is the institution about which few people talk and about which little is done in America. We go on today trying in educational, economic, governmental, and political ways to solve problems that are rooted in the home. I do not mean that these other efforts are insincere or even unneeded, but they will never deal fully with the problem of an unloved child, a child who has not learned discipline or work, and the resultant tragedy that so often occurs.

The time will come, but not soon enough, when the world may look at the principle of chastity and see what happens to people born out of wedlock who never know their father. Then men will begin to be concerned with that kind of root cause. You cannot study the life of Adolf Hitler and not be aware of the great embarrassment this twisted man felt in connection with the illegitimacy connected with his father.

We pay a price when we violate the basic spiritual laws, just as surely as we pay a price when we violate the physical laws of nature. This is why we must lovingly and tolerantly resist the blandishments of those who would try to give the world temporary comfort by giving it a massage when what it really needs is splints for broken bones and broken spirits (which, in my judgment, can come only from the gospel) and why we must resist temporary solutions that are really not solutions at all. Not only do they fail, but they deter many people from realizing that there are real solutions and that palliatives simply do not work.

My fourth point is how grateful I am to belong to a church in which there is a gospel that focuses on preventive medicine as well as redemptive medicine. The gospel really places heavy weight on the individual and his ultimate challenge to govern himself according to righteous principles. It rests on changing the inner man, not on changing outward circumstances—a slow and unglamorous way to lift the quality of life on this planet. What the world wants to do is to impose new outer control on man—more laws, more controls, more ways to chain us so we will not hurt each other. But as Edmund Burke wisely observed years and years ago, nobody can really be free who cannot checkrein his own appetites, because his passions "forge his fetters." A world that seeks to chain itself to keep from hurting each other, while at the same time resisting the very message that would help to change the inner man, must comprise one of the great paradoxes of our time. Fortunately the gospel also gives us what each of us needs—redemptive medicine when we fail and fall short. It is the wise interplay of prevention and redemption that makes the gospel of Jesus Christ the only solution to the human ills about which I know anything at all.

If you sometimes wonder if you are doing enough, and none of us is, it might be wise to contemplate the fact that the ninety-nine sheep that were relatively secure makes it possible for the shepherd to look for the lost sheep. It is the very fact that many have greater comparative spiritual health that permits us to do anything at all for the few who are in deep trouble. The preventive dimension of the gospel often gets overlooked because what I call the conspicuous Christianity, the glamorous and good causes, often overshadows the quiet Christianity that brings into our lives the preventive medicine, permitting us to help and to search for the lost sheep.

I believe that sin is a special form of insanity and that it reflects a kind of "blackout" in which we either lack perspective about the consequences of our thoughts, words, and actions or we lose it temporarily. Thus, all of us in small ways (and some in gross ways) lose our sense of perspective about the consequences of what we do. We would not really hurt people as much as we do if we knew the ultimate cost and price we all pay. All of us in our own way must have words we would recall if we could and acts we would not have done if we had the choice to make over now that we have seen the consequences. It is that lack of perspective that causes much sin—but not all, for some sin is sheer defiance. Part of what the gospel attempts to do is to give us a perspective about each other that will reduce the tendency we have to hurt.

Sixth, you are in some peer groups in which there is an almost constant celebration of the senses—tactile, visual, and aural. It has been significant to me that four prophets in four different cultures and in four different times each used the same two words to describe a people who had celebrated the senses so much that they had lost their capacity to feel. The words *past feeling* appear at these four different points in the scriptures to describe people who had become so sufficiently encrusted in their excesses that they had killed their capacity to feel; the very capacity to feel that they celebrated was lost in the process of celebration. They were in the situation in which stronger and stronger doses of this or that were needed in order to feel anything, and finally no dose was large enough.

If we care about our capacity to feel for people, for beauty, for life, for nature, this imposes upon us a self-discipline to keep that capacity alive and not to become encrusted in the excesses about which I have spoken.

Seventh, it is a useful perception at times in the quietude of our own ponderings to remember that the strait and narrow path that calls us to love, to forgive, to be chaste, to render service, to focus on basic things, is in a sense a heroic path to travel. It is not where the multitudes move, and what makes that path unpopulous is that only the brave care to try to climb it. It is not crowded on the west slope of Everest, for most people prefer the foothills. They need our help. We can help them best by not abandoning our role as guides to the strait and narrow way but by directing traffic thereto.

In this context C. S. Lewis said very wisely that bad people do not know anything about temptation because they have never resisted it. They always give in. Jesus, who descended below all things, was the most tempted of any person ever to live on the face of this earth. He can tell us about temptation because he knew how strong it was and how strong it can become—*because* he resisted it! You will not learn anything about temptation from bad people. You cannot feel how strong the wind is when you lie down; it is when you walk against it and move against it—then you know. In the same way, we must not expect any messages about the thrills and satisfactions of traveling the strait and narrow from those who do not walk that path at all.

Next, I am more firmly persuaded than ever, as a result of these last few months, that we cannot prevail individually without cultivating our capacity for individual revelation and inspiration, however difficult that may sound. The men whom I admire most have made a special point of cultivating this capacity to receive the extra dimension of guidance that comes through the gift of the Holy Ghost. I have seen the First Presidency and the Twelve several times in the last few months, in matters with which I had some affinity, humbly draw on a divine data bank for correct answers, not fully understanding the implications of the answers they received, but following the answers obediently because they knew the source of those answers and that they were correct. That takes not only humility, but it takes courage to follow. If we are to be secure, that must be our style too.

Sometimes I think when we are not ripe with experience, we may feel that personal revelation is still something to be developed later in life. I like what our just-departed and very wise Richard L. Evans said about how the earliest one can ever begin to change is *now* and the only place from which we can begin is *here*. The "here and now" of that challenge is to develop our capacity to deepen our relationship with our Father in heaven in order to receive his guidance. There are so many circumstances you will enter in which the institution of the Church cannot be with you. Brother Evans also noted that there comes a time when youth are left to themselves alone. We can better face such times, in my judgment, if we develop an appreciation for the scriptures. Even if you and I could just find ten or fifteen minutes a week to look for insights that are particularly germane to our lives at this point, how great a blessing that would be! A few examples follow.

I am intrigued by the concept in Revelation in which God describes this as a "living" church and what he might convey by that word. As I talk with medical men and others about what constitutes the presence of life, and add a few ideas of my own, I get these ideas: A living church would be a church whose doctrines, revelations, and insights are still growing. It is not closed conceptually. It is open-ended. Indeed, the Church is a living church. Something is also thought to be living when it responds to stimuli and the process of life, either when its existence is threatened by trends or developments or when it responds to the needs of those it serves; and thus the Church must view with alarm some trends of our time. It must also seek to serve and respond to feedback and stimuli that flow to it from its members.

A living church would still be growing and replicating itself—it would have capacity to reproduce. Indeed, this is happening internationally, and you will live to see the time when the verse in the 90th section of the Doctrine and Covenants will be fulfilled (and some of you will help fulfill it), for the gospel will be heard by every man "in his own language and in his own tongue." That could not be done by a church that is not living and replicating itself in countless cultures.

A living church would also be one in which there is movement and action. Mormonism is not a religion of repose. It is not monastic. Of course there are times when you and I would like to have a little moment for reflection, and we sometimes get "hustled" organizationally. But the gospel of Jesus Christ closes with life; it does not lean away from life.

Finally a living church would be one that stays connected with the ultimate sources of power in the universe,
lest it grow cold conceptually and in every other way. Individually and institutionally, we must stay connected with
the superintelligences who have found how to prevail in this
cold universe and prevail happily.

May I suggest what seem to me to be examples of things
in the scriptures that are germane to your concerns, to the
concerns of youth everywhere. There are scriptural under-
pinnings that suggest you are right to be concerned about
the stewardship for this planet, its beauty and its resources.
You ought to know what they are. There are scriptures that
say what I hear you saying in some of your best moments as
a generation—that we need to be closer to nature. In the
88th section of the Doctrine and Covenants we are asked to
contemplate the heavens, and we are promised that if we do
we will have "seen God moving in his majesty."

Your generation rightly says a lot about love. The only
love worthy of the word is unconditional love, including, as
the scriptures say, "love unfeigned." We are told to "level"
with each other about our generation, and I agree. There are
a half dozen places in the scriptures where we are told to level
with each other in the context of love—and then, as Jesus
says, we "gain" our brother.

We are told that poverty is not good, that sharp economic despair is a major source of sin in the world. And
while we are warned about the greed of the rich, we are
also warned about the greed of the poor. It is almost as
though, in terms of current concerns as real as poverty is,
we have now reached the point Dostoevsky foresaw when he
said the time would come when secular sages would say,
"There is no crime. There is no sin. There is only hunger."
Indeed there is hunger, but there is also crime and there is
sin. The scriptures give us a balanced approach to poverty
through the gospel of work, which provides the ultimate
parameters for the solution of poverty. The scriptures also

tell us that freedom by itself is not enough, not without purpose and perspective, for being free by itself becomes a kind of vast desert in which each of us finds himself not knowing what to do or what to respond to. The sense of existential despair seems to deepen in western civilizations each passing day for that and many other reasons.

You are rightly concerned in the abuse of political power. The Doctrine and Covenants says it is the nature of "almost all men" to abuse power. One of the fortunate things in the Church is that we get experience receiving and administering with power early in life. How fortuitous that is!

The scriptures also tell us it is "not good for man to be alone," and the piles of sociological and behavioral data confirm that with a shout. The isolate is not only miserable himself, but he will take many others "under" with him.

The scriptures tell us about the thrill of orthodoxy, the balancing of these dangerous doctrines of Christ that need each other just as the people of Christ need each other in order to be balanced and to produce happiness. That high adventure of orthodoxy takes great courage.

The scriptures also tell us about war—that it exists "in the hearts and minds of our countrymen," perhaps not just as pertained to the Civil War but now too.

The scriptures tell us that there are those that would manipulate our appetites—that we should not be so naive as to assume that there are not evil men with "designs which will exist in the hearts of conspiring men in the last days."

The scriptures tell us the cosmetic solutions to the human problems will not work, because there is "none other way" except to follow the Savior.

I believe, my young brothers and sisters, that if we are serious about the scriptures, they will give each of us the touches of inspiration and guidance that are crucial to our happiness in the decision-making each of us must perform. We are told to select "good causes." That takes judgment and some inspiration. We are told to do things "of our own free will" and to be anxious about them.

In closing, may I suggest some lines from C. S. Lewis in which he wrote about our need to build a deeper personal relationship with our Father in heaven—not to keep him at arm's length, but to let him in our lives so he can work with us and "rebuild" us. Lewis says:

> Imagine yourself as a living house. God comes in to rebuild that house. At first, perhaps, you can understand what He is doing. He is getting the drains right and stopping the leaks in the roofs, and so on. You knew that those jobs needed doing and so you are not surprised. But presently, He starts knocking the house about in a way that hurts abominably and does not seem to make sense. What on earth is He up to? The explanation is that He is building quite a different house from the one you thought of, throwing out a wing here, putting on an extra floor there, running up new towers, making courtyards. You thought you were going to be made into a decent little cottage, but He is building a palace. (*Mere Christianity.*)

If we are not serious about that kind of relationship, it will not happen. If we simply want to be "decent little cottages," that can be arranged. But the thrill of the greater adventure seems to me to be the one that the gospel summons you and me to. May God bless you with a quiet sense of destiny, not with hubris or arrogance, but with a realization, at least in part, of what lies ahead of you, having been ushered onto the stage of life at this critical point in the history of the Church. Prepare yourselves secularly and spiritually, but remember that there is an increasing death rate for the mortal concepts in secular education. The decreasing longevity of many mortal concepts is a function of the discovery and turbulence of knowledge. Remember that you and I would do well to anchor ourselves to unchanging things, the things that serve us now and will serve us a million years from now—the things that really matter.

This is the Church of him whose name it bears. The youth of the Church in some lands may perhaps be less sophisticated than they are in others, but they all march with the Church, they are all equally committed, and they are all vital to the cultures and the countrymen they seek to serve.

May God bless youth everywhere with that quiet sense of destiny, I pray in the name of him whose Church this is, Jesus Christ. Amen.

Peace—
Whither?

David H. Yarn, Jr.

DAVID H. YARN, JR., is professor of philosophy at Brigham Young University, where he has been a faculty member for more than 20 years. He is also a member of the faculty advisory council. He has been chairman of the department of theology and philosophy, and was the first Dean of the College of Religious Instruction.

Dr. Yarn holds the B.A. degree from BYU, and the M.A. and Ed.D. degrees from Columbia University in the City of New York.

He has written three books, co-edited another, and has chapters or major sections in six other books. He has been honored in educational and Church circles, and in 1966 was the recipient of the Karl G. Maeser Award for Teaching Excellence.

He currently serves as president of the BYU 8th Stake of the Church, and has been a missionary, high councilor, bishop, counselor in stake presidencies, and has served on the general boards of the YMMIA and Sunday School.

His wife is the former Marilyn Stevenson, and they are the parents of six daughters.

PEACE—WHITHER?

David H. Yarn, Jr.

In Thomas Hobbes' political classic, *Leviathan*, published in 1651, we have a significant comment on peace. It occurs in a context in which Hobbes discusses his concept of the nature of man, and describes what he calls the causes of quarrel. Then he says:

> Hereby it is manifest, that during the time men live without a common power to keep them all in awe, they are in that condition which is called war; and such a war, as is of every man, against every man. For war, consisteth not in battle only, or the act of fighting; but in a tract of time, wherein the will to contend by battle is sufficiently known: and therefore the notion of *time*, is to be considered in the nature of war; as it is in the nature of weather. For as the nature of foul weather, lieth not in a shower or two of rain; but in an inclination thereto of many days together; so the nature of war, consisteth not in actual fighting; but in the known disposition thereto, during all the time there is no assurance to the contrary. All other time is peace.[1]

This is a significant comment on peace because it reveals that in Hobbes' view the natural condition of man, or perhaps it is not inaccurate in light of history to say the usual condition of man, is that of war, especially as Hobbes so graphically described what since the mid-twentieth century has been called cold war. Peace then is, in effect, described negatively as the absence of war. His statement identifies peace as the absence of conflict between political powers and the absence of conflict between individuals.

Centuries before Hobbes there were other philosophers who also were concerned with the subject of peace. In fact,

---

[1]*Leviathan,* part I, chap. 13.

there were three major ancient schools of philosophy that were contemporary with each other and had a special interest in peace. Though their roots lay in an earlier period, the schools became prominent after the death of Alexander the Great and the political and military conflicts that destroyed or fragmented his empire. The schools were the Epicureans, the Stoics, and the Skeptics.

Although Epicureanism was to become a very degenerate pleasure philosophy, its founder, Epicurus, was basically a temperate and high-minded person whose principal concern was what he called the health of the soul. He tried to develop a philosophy that he thought would provide men with *ataraxia,* or freedom from pain in the body and freedom from disturbance in the mind. Thus men could live in a condition of peace.

In one passage where he speaks of this end, Epicurus expressly rejects the sensuality of which his system was accused and of which in decades and centuries after his death those who claimed his name were guilty:

> When, therefore, we maintain that pleasure is the end, we do not mean the pleasures of profligates and those that consist in sensuality, as is supposed by some who are either ignorant or disagree with us or do not understand, but freedom from pain in the body and from trouble in the mind. For it is not continuous drinkings and revellings, nor the satisfactions of lusts, nor the enjoyment of fish and other luxuries of the wealthy table, which produce a pleasant life, but sober reasoning, searching out the motives for all choice and avoidance, and banishing mere opinions, to which are due the greatest disturbance of the spirit.[2]

Like the Epicureans, the Stoics also sought peace of mind, but in a different way. They contended that the Epicureans were too dependent upon external circumstances, and they, on the contrary, said peace of mind was entirely independent of one's physical, economic, social, and political circumstances. Peace, they said, lay in doing one's duty and

---

[2]"Letters to Menoeceus" in *The Stoic and Epicurean Philosophers*, ed. W. J. Oates, p. 32.

was essentially the fruit of will. Epictetus said, "God created all men for happiness and peace of mind," and "the essence of good and of evil lies in an attitude of the will."[3]

There is but one way to peace of mind (keep this thought by you at dawn and in the day-time and at night)—to give up what is beyond your control, to count nothing your own, to surrender everything to heaven and fortune, to leave everything to be managed by those to whom Zeus has given control, and to devote yourself to one object only, that which is your own beyond all hindrance, and in all that you read and write and hear to make this your aim.[4]

Another champion of the Stoic concept of apathy, or indifference to the external world and dependence upon one's own will to do his duty was Marcus Aurelius, who counseled, "Be cheerful also, and seek not external help nor the tranquility which others give. A man then must stand erect, not be kept erect by others."[5]

An excellent representative statement of the goal of peace, as conceived by the Stoics, is this one from Marcus Aurelius, as he describes that which is peculiar to the good man:

To be pleased and content with what happens, and with the thread which is spun for him; and not to defile the divinity which is planted in his breast, nor disturb it by a crowd of images, but to preserve it tranquil, following it obediently as a god, neither saying anything contrary to the truth, nor doing anything contrary to justice. And if all men refuse to believe that he lives a simple, modest, and contented life, he is neither angry with any of them, nor does he deviate from the way which leads to the end of life, to which a man ought to come pure, tranquil, ready to depart, and without any compulsion perfectly reconciled to his lot.[6]

In addition to the Epicureans and Stoics, the Skeptics had a special interest in peace. Although the meaning that

---

[3]*Discourses*, book III, chap. 24; book I, chap. 29.
[4]Ibid., book IV, chap. 4.
[5]*Meditations*, 3:5.
[6]Ibid., 3:16.

is now probably most frequently associated with the word
skeptic is some form of the word *doubt,* those ancient
ones who were identified with the Greek word *skeptikoi*
were not considered "doubters," but "inquirers" or "investi-
gators." It might be said in truth that they were in the mainstream of workers trying to develop what in subsequent ages
was to be called scientific method. They formed strenuous
objections to the intellectual positions of thinkers in other
philosophical schools and resolved on what they considered
purely speculative propositions to maintain a suspension of
judgment.

Sextus Empiricus, the ancient historian of Skepticism,
says,

> The originating cause of Scepticism is, we say, the hope of attaining
> quietude. Men of talent, who were perturbed by the contradictions in
> things and in doubt as to which of the alternatives they ought to accept,
> were led on to inquire what is true in things and what false, hoping by
> the settlement of this question to attain quietude. The main basic prin-
> ciple of the Sceptic system is that of opposing to every proposition
> an equal proposition; for we believe that as a consequence of this we
> end by ceasing to dogmatize.[7]

In another place he says, "Hence we say that, while in
regard to matters of opinion the Sceptic's End is quietude, in
regard to things unavoidable it is 'moderate affection.' "[8]

It is a matter of no small interest that those ancient
scientists and philosophers of science, the Skeptics, were
limpid clear in declaring that the "originating cause of Scep-
ticism" was the "hope of attaining quietude," or what we
more commonly call peace. To be sure that his readers understood his meaning, Sextus Empiricus defined *quietude* as
"an untroubled and tranquil condition of soul."[9]

Perhaps the practical implications of the position of the
ancient Skeptics is no better illustrated than in this brief

----

[7]*Outlines of Pyrrhonism,* book I, chap. 6.
[8]Ibid., book I, chap. 12.
[9]Ibid., book I, chap. 6 and chap. 4.

counsel Lucian puts in the mouth of his fabled character, Tiresias, when Menippus visited him in Hades, the realm of the dead, seeking an answer to the question, "What is the best life?"

The life of the ordinary man is the best and most prudent choice; cease from the folly of metaphysical speculation and inquiry into origins and ends, utterly reject their clever logic, count all these things idle talk, and pursue one end alone—how you may do what your hand finds to do, and go your way with ever a smile and never a passion.[10]

Hobbes, as a political philosopher, saw peace principally as a relationship between states and between individuals. But the ethical philosophers, the Epicureans, Stoics, and Skeptics, thought of peace principally as an internal condition in the the soul of an individual.

One philosophical characterization of our own century is found in the phrase "The Age of Analysis." It has become the century without equal in terms of massive scientific and technological creativity; physical, economic, and social mobility; mass education; almost omnipresent voices of communications media; vast urbanization of society, etc.—all of which in their own ways have not only served mankind, but have created almost numberless pressures, problems, circumstances, conditions, threats, desires, and temptations to challenge character, undermine the family, and even destroy the self.

Many *isms* and *ologies* have been part of this vast complex development, one of the most prominent and influential of which being psychology. And as, from a philosophical point of view, this century has been called the age of analysis, it may with good reason, from a psychological point of view, be called the age of psychoanalysis.

It is a matter of considerable interest that the science of psychology and psychoanalysis came into being when men were merely on the threshold of this century, with all of its

---

[10]"Menippus," from Lucian of Samosata's *Dialogues of the Dead.*

self-fragmenting influences. As valuable as analysis can be, no doubt, analysis alone perpetuates the problem of fragmentation, when what men have needed is synthesis, something that unifies the parts and gives meaning and purpose to the whole.

Joshua Loth Leibman relates the following personal experience:

> Once, as a young man full of exuberant fancy, I undertook to draw up a catalogue of the acknowledged "goods" of life. As other men sometimes tabulate lists of properties they own or would like to own, I set down my inventory of earthly desirables: health, love, beauty, talent, power, riches, and fame—together with several minor ingredients of what I considered man's perfect portion.
>
> When my inventory was completed I proudly showed it to a wise elder who had been the mentor and spiritual model of my youth. Perhaps I was trying to impress him with my precocious wisdom and the large universality of my interests. Anyway, I handed him the list. "This," I told him confidently, "is the sum of mortal goods. Could a man possess them all, he would be as a god."
>
> At the corners of my friend's old eyes, I saw wrinkles of amusement gathering in a patient net. "An excellent list," he said, pondering it thoughtfully. "Well digested in content and set down in not-unreasonable order. But it appears, my young friend, that you have omitted the most important element of all. You have forgotten the one ingredient lacking which each possession becomes a hideous torment, and your list as a whole an intolerable burden."
>
> "And what," I asked, peppering my voice with truculence, "is that missing ingredient?"
>
> With a pencil stub he crossed out my entire schedule. Then, having demolished my adolescent dream structure at a single stroke, he wrote down three syllables: *peace of mind*.
>
> "This is the gift that God reserves for His special proteges," he said. "Talent and beauty He gives to many. Wealth is commonplace, fame not rare. But peace of mind—that is His final guerdon of approval, the fondest sign of His love. He bestows it charily. Most men are never blessed with it; others wait all their lives—yes, far into advanced age—for this gift to descend upon them."[11]

----

[11]*Peace of Mind* (New York: Simon and Schuster, 1946), pp. 3-4.

No doubt there are many persons who are part of the present maddening confusion in the world who would cry out, "Peace of mind! What's peace of mind? How could anybody have peace of mind?" They have been unable to find it in the philosophies of the ancients or moderns. They do not know where to look. Although great minds have contemplated international peace, interpersonal peace, and innerpersonal peace, all mankind has known is conflict.

Since the fall of man, strife has been abroad in the earth in the forms of both inter and inner conflicts. But contrary to what the world may think, from that time the Lord has provided men with the means whereby they could know peace if they would. When Adam was taught the ordinance of baptism and the role of the water, the blood, and the spirit, he was told by the Lord:

> Therefore it is given to abide in you; the record of heaven; the Comforter; the peaceable things of immortal glory; the truth of all things; that which quickeneth all things, which maketh alive all things; that which knoweth all things, and hath all power, according to wisdom, mercy, truth, justice, and judgment.
>
> And now, behold, I say unto you: This is the plan of salvation unto all men, through the blood of mine Only Begotten, who shall come in the meridian of time. (Moses 6:61-62.)

From the days of Adam sacrifices and burnt offerings were made to the Lord, which, among other things, kept the Lord, the Source of peace, before the minds of the people.

When Moses was given instruction on Sinai, the Lord gave him commandments regarding sacrifices and offerings, and among them one of the most commonly observed, the peace offerings. It is not insignificant that the word for peace offering, *shelem*, is derived from a root word, *shalam*, which, among other things, means "to make peaceable, or be at peace, that is to perfect, to recompense, to make restitution, to restore, and to reward." Even a moment's reflection suggests connections between these meanings and the Messiah, who makes those things possible, and who is the Source of peace.

The scriptures suggest that Isaiah had a profound understanding of the mission of the Messiah, and that genuine peace was inextricably dependent upon him. He described in part the peaceful circumstances which will obtain during the millennium, when the Messiah will reign; and among his prophecies concerning the Messiah, who was yet to come, is this declaration of some of the names by which He would be known:

> For unto us a child is born, unto us a son is given: and the government shall be upon his shoulder: and his name shall be called Wonderful, Counseller, The mighty God, The everlasting Father, The Prince of Peace. (Isaiah 9:6.)

The Prince of Peace is a particularly fascinating title and has a remarkably illuminating counterpart given in modern revelation. It is related to the long disputed New Testament phrase Son of Man. In revelation given to the Prophet Joseph Smith it was manifested that one of the names of God is Man of Holiness (Moses 6:57). This means, of course, that the Christ is the Son of Man of Holiness. Consequently, Son of Man is an abbreviated form of the full name Son of Man of Holiness. Inasmuch as peace is the fruit of holiness, it is evident that there is a significant relationship between the phrase Son of Man of Holiness and Isaiah's the Prince of Peace.

The Gospel of Luke declares that when the infant Christ came into the world, a multitude of the heavenly host bore witness of him praising God and saying: "Glory to God in the highest, and on earth peace, good will toward men." (Luke 2:14.)

When John the Baptist was born, his father, Zacharias, was filled with the Holy Ghost and prophecied about his own son who would prepare the way for the Lord, who would:

> . . . Give light to them that sit in darkness and in the shadow of death, to guide our feet into the way of peace. (Luke 1:79.)

In the last discourses the mortal Lord gave to his apostles, he said:

> Peace I leave with you, my peace I give unto you: not as the world giveth, give I unto you. . . . (John 14:27.)

As he concluded these discourses, the Lord declared:

> These things I have spoken unto you, that in me ye might have peace. In the world ye shall have tribulation. . . . (John 16:33.)

The Lord prophecied on several occasions that his disciples would experience hardships, persecutions, and often the hatred of the world, but at the same time he assured them of his peace—a peace the world could not give. The world would even give them tribulation (the opposite of external peace), but because of him and his gospel they would have inner peace.

Although he was and is the Prince of Peace, he was explicit that because many would reject him when others, even of their own families, accepted him, the external result would often be division. Symbolic of the destruction which would come as a consequence of the conflict he said in one place, "Think not that I am come to send peace on earth: I came not to send peace, but a sword." (Matthew 10:34; also see Luke 12:51.)

The Apostle Paul was sorely tried for his faith and was in a position to know the tribulation of which the Lord had spoken, but he, more importantly, knew the peace of the Master.

As Paul wrote to the saints, instructing and encouraging them, he said:

For the kingdom of God is not meat and drink; but righteousness, and peace, and joy in the Holy Ghost.

Let us therefore follow after the things which make for peace, and things wherewith one may edify another. (Romans 14:17, 19.)

Or, seeking the essence of the words of Paul, he bids mankind to follow after the things which make for peace, "for the kingdom of God is righteousness, and peace, and joy in the Holy Ghost."

Before the Fall the earth was in a terrestrial state or a condition of peace, and during the millennium it will be returned to a terrestrial state, or a condition of peace. But it is presently in a telestial state, inhabited by many men and women who will live only a telestial law. And as long as the earth is in a telestial state, having among its inhabitants those who will be sons of perdition and those who refuse to live more than a telestial law, permanent external peace is not a genuine universal possibility.

The Lord, knowing the perverseness of mankind, gave Joseph Smith a revelation on 25 December 1832, in which he declared that from the commencement of the conflict he described, which is now known as the Civil War, "war shall be poured out upon all nations," accompanied by violence in the forces of nature, "until the consumption decreed hath made a full end of all nations; That the cry of the saints, and of the blood of the saints, shall cease to come up into the ears of the Lord of Sabaoth [Hosts], from the earth, to be avenged of their enemies. Wherefore, stand ye in holy places, and be not moved, until the day of the Lord come; for behold, it cometh quickly, saith the Lord. Amen." (D&C 87:1-8.)

But, it was also because the Lord knew the recalcitrance of mankind, as well as because of his love for them, that he had restored the gospel and charged those whom he authorized to go throughout the world calling mankind to repentance, giving man the opportunity to receive the message of exaltation and to obtain inner peace, that is, "to enjoy the words of eternal life in this world, and eternal life in the world to come, even immortal glory." (Moses 6:59.)

And, although the fallen world has always known international conflicts, inter-personal conflicts, and inner-personal conflicts, there have been those both before and after Jesus who, through him, have known his peace by accepting him and his redeeming gospel in their lives.

The people of Enoch not only knew inner peace, but external peace also, "And the Lord called his people Zion, because they were of one heart and one mind, and dwelt in righteousness; and there was no poor among them." (Moses 7:18.)

Another people who really accepted the Lord, and not merely gave assent to him, received the blessings incident to their acceptance. They were the Nephites after the Lord's resurrection, visit among them, and ascension.

> And it came to pass that there was no contention in the land, because of the love of God which did dwell in the hearts of the people.
>
> And there were no envyings, nor strifes, nor tumults, nor whoredoms, nor lyings, nor murders, nor any manner of lasciviousness; and surely there could not be a happier people among all the people who had been created by the hand of God.
>
> There were no robbers, nor murderers, neither were there Lamanites, nor any manner of -ites; but they were in one, the children of Christ, and heirs to the kingdom of God.
>
> And how blessed were they! For the Lord did bless them in all their doings; yea, even they were blessed and prospered until an hundred and ten years had passed away; and the first generation from Christ had passed away, and there was no contention in all the land. (4 Nephi 15-18.)

Just as accepting the Lord and his righteousness has brought inner peace into the lives of individuals, and inter-personal peace into the groups of individuals who mutually live in righteousness, so the living of his gospel would bring peace among all men, if all mankind would truly accept him. In view of the corruption with which mankind is almost constantly bombarded from practically every quarter, and the unstable and inflammable political conditions which seem to prevail so universally, one would almost proclaim, as it was declared of many of Adam's posterity in the early age of the world, "they loved Satan more than God." (Moses 5:13.)

The actions and words of multitudes do trumpet to the world in almost deafening voice that they love Satan more than God, and that includes many so-called peace advocates and some others who, though perhaps well-meaning, are looking for peace where it is not to be found.

The authorized servants of the Lord, and all who have made covenants with the Lord through the administrations of his authorized servants, are charged in modern revelation to inform others of the gospel, and to warn them of the calamities which sinful men are bringing upon the world. For the Lord has said:

> Behold, I sent you out to testify and warn the people, and it becometh every man who hath been warned to warn his neighbor. (D&C 88:81.)

And also:

> But learn that he who doeth the works of righteousness shall receive his reward, even peace in this world, and eternal life in the world to come. (D&C 59:23.)

Permanent world peace is not a genuine possibility as long as this world is permeated with telestial influences; nevertheless man must continue to pursue it; and though the pursuit of universal world peace will continue to fail because righteousness is not a sufficient part of that pursuit, the Source of true peace will continuously be born witness of in the world to those who have eyes to see, and ears to hear, and hearts that understand, and they shall have peace.

To some extent Paul saw the consequences of this in his own ministry. For example, he said this to the Ephesians:

But now in Christ Jesus ye who sometimes were far off are made nigh by the blood of Christ.

For he is our peace, who hath made both one, and hath broken down the middle wall of partition between us;

Having abolished in his flesh the enmity, even the law of commandments contained in ordinances; for to make in himself of twain one new man, so making peace;

And that he might reconcile both unto God in one body by the cross, having slain the enmity thereby:

And came and preached peace to you which were afar off, and to them that were nigh.

For through him we both have access by one Spirit unto the Father.

Now therefore ye are no more strangers and foreigners, but fellow-citizens with the saints, and of the household of God;

And are built upon the foundation of the apostles and prophets, Jesus Christ himself being the chief corner stone. . . . (Ephesians 2:13-20.)

Just as Paul saw the Jew and gentile eliminate the barriers which had existed between them when they jointly came unto Christ, and as we have seen men and women from all nations in our own time come unto the Christ and his restored gospel, we shall continue to see barriers eliminated and see at least in part what it is like for man to be one as we come to Christ.

We do live in a time of great conflict and turmoil in men, between men, between groups of men, between men and women, between youth and adults, between the self-proclaimed new generation and the "old" generation, between races, between nations, and groups of nations. And although conflict and turmoil are a reality, peace is also a reality. Inter-national peace, inter-personal peace, and inner-personal peace are available to all of those who are willing to bring to the Source of peace that which is required of them.

And the peace of God, which passeth all understanding, shall keep your hearts and minds through Christ Jesus. (Philippians 4:7.)

Man
Illumined

Truman G. Madsen

TRUMAN G. MADSEN has contributed greatly to thinking and writing in the Church. He is known far and wide as a brilliant lecturer and as a defender of the faith. He has attained excellence in the academic world, and has given superior service in ecclesiastical positions.

Presently he is professor of religion and philosophy at Brigham Young University. He obtained his B.S. and M.S. degrees at the University of Utah, and then studied at the University of Southern California. He spent four years at Harvard working for A.M. and Ph.D. degrees. He completed two doctoral examinations, and his thesis was termed "one of the finest to be written by any candidate in the school's history."

He has written and published widely in books, pamphlets, and magazines.

In the Church he has been a bishop, was president of the New England Mission, and is now a member of the Sunday School general board.

He and his wife Ann have three children.

MAN ILLUMINED

Truman G. Madsen

The sum of this essay can be put in one word: *Light.*
We see with and through light; but we rarely turnabout to
examine light—itself. Yet continually why and what and
how questions are put to me which, I am convinced, are less
questions than they are questings, questings for Light.

No theme is more central to modern revelation than
light "that lighteth every man that cometh into the world."
(John 10:10.) The Church itself came "out of obscurity and
darkness" into the light, and the light of modern revelation
centers in Christ. Consider the following excerpts:

> That which is of God is light. (D&C 50:24.)
>
> That which doth not edify [lift, inspire, enliven] is not of God and
> is darkness. (D&C 50:13.)
>
> He that ascended up on high, as also he descended below all things,
> in that he comprehended all things, that he might be in all and through
> all things, the light of truth. (D&C 88:6.)
>
> And the light which shineth, which giveth you light, is through
> him who enlighteneth your eyes, which is the same light that quickeneth
> your understandings. (D&C 88:11.)
>
> Truth embraceth truth; virtue loveth virtue; light cleaveth unto
> light [as darkness cleaveth unto darkness]. (D&C 88:40.)
>
> Light and truth forsake [detect and withdraw from] that evil one.
> (D&C 93:37.)   ,
>
> Christ's light is *in* all things: It . . . giveth life to all things
> ["maketh alive all things" (Moses 6:61)] . . . is through all things
> [surrounds, envelops, permeates] . . . is the law by which all things are
> governed. (D&C 88:13, 41.)
>
> And if your eye be single [constantly upreaching and outreaching]
> to his glory, your whole bodies shall be filled with light, and there shall

be no darkness in you. And that body which is filled with light comprehendeth all things. (D&C 88:67.)

Then shall ye know that ye have seen [Christ (indirectly in the
light of sun, moon, and stars, but directly in a former condition of glory
in his presence)], that I am, and that I am the true light that is in you,
and that you are in me; otherwise ye could not abound [that is, live,
grow, flourish]. (D&C 88:50.)

Every man whose spirit receiveth not the light is under condemnation. For man is spirit. (D&C 93:32-33.)

And that which was from the beginning is plainly manifest unto
them, and they receive not the light. (D&C 93:31.)

He that keepeth his commandments receiveth truth and light, until
he is glorified in truth and knoweth all things. (D&C 93:28.)

He that receiveth light and continueth in God receiveth more light,
and that light groweth brighter and brighter until the perfect day [the
day of perfect light, the light of the perfect day]. (D&C 50:24.) *

From these revelatory and sweeping insights into the
nature of light and the light of nature, one senses the beginnings of the whole cosmology, a prodigious and unifying
key to the secrets of the vast universe. I select only those
themes that apply to man himself, his makeup, his comprehension, his life fulfillment.

Light as the Real

These revelations suggest that man is more than a re-
ceptacle of degrees of light, he is somehow in his very primal
makeup composed of light. One associate of the Prophet
Joseph Smith understood him to say "that light or spirit, and
matter, are the two great primary principles of the universe,
or of Being; that they are self-existent, co-existent, inde-
structible and eternal and from these two elements, both
our spirits and our bodies were formulated."[1]

It is implicit in this statement that "pure light" (if that
means unembodied light) is somehow less advanced than the

---

*Of all scripture, this is the favorite passage of President Joseph Fielding
Smith.
[1]Letter of Benjamin F. Johnson to George Gibbs, p. 7, in Church Historian's Office.

living light that comes in the complex organization of spirit bodies and physical bodies—could we say "light magnified"? Yet he adds:

Light and heat . . . fill the immensity of space, and permeate with latent life, and heat, every particle of which all works and composed.[2]

Light and heat are, even in their grosser forms, refining and welding influences. But the light and heat in the fusion of realities that is man transcend somehow the lesser and grosser forms of light.

Light as Truth

If, then, light is interfused with man's spirit and physical bodies, we may see how fitting it is to say that light is truth. The glorified Christ says, "I *am* the Truth." Elsewhere he speaks of himself as "the spirit of Truth" and in the same vein "the light of truth." And again as "Intelligence, or the light of truth," and says, "I am more intelligent than they all," more intelligent, that is, than all other intelligences.

Truth in one sense is, as our hymn says, "the sum of existence." It is another name for reality, that which is. But in a second sense, "truth is knowledge" (D&C 93:24), the accurate perception of that which is. Christ himself has become the truth in both senses. First, he is the fulness of personality: he is the sum of human existence. Second, he illumines the truth for us. By experiencing the struggle toward perfection, he "descended below all things" (into darkness that "comprehended him not"). Thus he received a fulness of the glory of the Father, which is a fulness of the light of God. And having made that light his own, he is the source for us of "the life and the light, the spirit and the power sent forth by the will of the Father" through him.

In mortality the more light one receives, the more he can receive. We grow and glow not just by addition but by

—————
[2]Ibid.

multiplication. Hence the promise, "Unto him that receiveth it shall be given more, even power" (D&C 71:6), and its correlative warning, "But whosoever continueth not to receive, from him shall be taken away, even that he hath." (Matt. 13:11 IV.) The more man increases in light, the more he gains access to truth and acquires intelligent consciousness of all that light penetrates—on the one hand, the immensity of space and, on the other hand, the immensity of time—"things as they are, and as they were, and as they are to come" (D&C 93:24). Eventually he may receive the fulness of light that circumscribes all truth.

Said Brigham Young:

> It is not the optic nerve alone that gives knowledge of surrounding objects to the mind but it is that which God has placed in man—a system of intelligence that attracts knowledge as light cleaves to light, intelligence to intelligence, and truth to truth. It is this which lays in man a proper foundation for all education. (*Discourses*, p. 277.)

When we are told, "If ye receive not the spirit ye shall not teach" (D&C 42:14), it means more than that we should not. We cannot. More—without it, we cannot even understand. "Why is it," the Lord asks, "that ye cannot understand and know, that he that receiveth the word by the Spirit of truth receiveth it as it is preached by the Spirit of truth? Wherefore, he that preacheth and he that receiveth, understand one another, and both are edified and rejoice together." (D&C 50:21-22.) Teaching any truth, even the most elemental or simple facts, is exciting to both teacher and student. Touched by the light, they tend to see the infusion, the "hand of God," as it were, everywhere.

> And I have felt
> A presence that disturbs me with the joy
> Of elevated thoughts; a sense sublime
> Of something far more deeply interfused.
> —Wordsworth[3]

---

[3]"Lines composed a few miles above Tintern Abbey."

But one who is yet to respond needs what the Prophet once referred to as a rebirth of one's eyes before he can see any difference between the kingdom of God and the kingdoms of the world. Such a one tends to see no light anywhere. Just as 20-20 vision is helpless without light, so, in the wider world of the spirit, the "eyes of the understanding" must be quickened.

Quickened carries at least three strands of meaning—"to enliven, to hasten, to permeate." Careful introspection will show that there is no mental process that is not intensified by the subtle enlightening process described by the Prophet—"when you feel pure intelligence flowing into you." (*Teachings*, p. 151.) Not only are there "sudden strokes," "a logical flow of ideas," the "first promptings," but also a brightening effect that enables us to see what we saw before, but now in quite literally a new light. The effects extend to the person as a whole—even his balance, coordination, and motor skills. In the understanding light has to do with the clarifying of concepts and judgments (more than analytic proficiency), with the heightening of imagination (more than aimless fantasy), with the recovery and interweaving of memories (more than chance deliverances of the subconscious), and with the strivings and inspirings of creativity. These phenomena take one beyond the "light barriers." His mental life is "brighter."

The teaching that our "whole bodies" can be full of light suggests that what we call "IQ" is a clumsy and misleading "measure" of man's cognitive powers. Genuine intelligence, or the conscious "light of truth," is the light that recognizes and absorbs or "cleaves" to truth, and it involves the whole man. Intelligence, in short, is a kind of light-susceptibility. Hence the Prophet needed a Urim and Thummim until he himself became one and was named by the Lord "seer" and "Gazelam" (a seer stone) (D&C 79:9). We have a glimpse of that level of light and burning in the Prophet as he emerged with Sidney Rigdon from his chamber, after they had written "while yet in the Spirit" a portion of what they had together beheld in "The Vision." His statement is "My whole body was full of light and I could see even out at the ends of my fingers and toes."[4]

We are reaching toward this awareness when we say, "I know with every fiber of my being." The scriptures are replete with testimony that the capacities, the hidden potential, the lava, of our inner responses to truth far exceed any plaudits ever offered for the "genius." We can no more "drink up the ocean" than we can learn all truth "line by line." But "that body which is filled with light comprehendeth all things," and the ocean, indeed all oceans, are subject to the rays that proceed from and return to him who is "glorified in truth" and "knoweth all things."

The principle "truth embraceth truth; virtue loveth virtue; light cleaveth unto light" (D&C 88:40), helps us explain many of the experiences of the religious struggle. For example:

How five minutes is sufficient to bring vibrant and total trust for one person, and fifty years not long enough for another, though the "evidence" or record is the same for both.

How the most intense sympathy, empathy, and social feelings emerge in settings of light and spiritual experience, a mutual kinship out of mutual kindling.

How enslaving habits and degenerate compulsions in the flesh, which stand like an impenetrable shield between the spirit of man and the Spirit of God, can be purged and purified—burned out—by a light-power that heals and redeems. And why "you can't change human nature" is simply false if "you" includes your spirit and Christ's Spirit power.

How light can be glaring and unpleasant, even blinding, when first we are subjected to it, but then the increasing intensities and heats become more than endurable; they render our former condition repugnant.

---

[4]Philo Dibble, *Faith Promoting Series*, VIII, 80-81.

How grosser light stops with surfaces and casts shadows, but the higher light can be in us and through us.

How we "receive the Spirit through prayer" (D&C 63:64), but also do not really pray until and unless we pray with the Spirit and "in the Spirit." (D&C 46:28-30.)

How there are two kinds of burning in us, one a burning of conscience, urging and lifting us to become what we have in us to become (and accumulating guilt in postponement), and second a burning of approval and peace when we set about repentance.

How negative feelings can restrain the peace and power of light as it flows down, yet how the flow of the Spirit can melt away all such dross if we will permit our spirits to "take the lead."

Light as the Good

If light is somehow the substratum of all reality and also of all intelligent awareness of reality, it is only another step to say that light is the foundation of good. In few, if any, ancient or modern cultures has "light" become symbolic of evil, "dark" of good. Instead, light tends to be identified with the good, the valuable, the blessed, the sacred. But it is more than a symbol or a ritual. The scriptures teach that the light of Christ is given to every man that cometh into the world, but that it enlightens "through the world" all those that hearken. Light edifies, lifts, and "that which does not edify is not of God and is darkness." That is the bound and condition of all law, physical and moral, the "law by which all things are governed" (D&C 88:13). Light is not just the test of good; it is the nature of all that is judged truly good. Alma, who had emerged from guilt-ridden darkness that made his own extinction seem desirable, wrote, "Whatsoever is light is good." (Alma 32:35.)

In the realm of the good, as elsewhere, light is the "bound and condition" of all preferred ways of life. And these bounds and conditions are inexorable and exceptionless, not because they tell us what our choices must be, but because they tell us what the *results* of our choices will be. Of course, one can attempt to "become a law unto himself," but only at the cost of diminishing the light. Every minute of every day we are increasing or decreasing in our receptivity to light, and there is no way to escape the inevitability of that consequence in our thoughts, our acts, our very breath. One can look upon the law of light either as the enemy of freedom or as freedom's guarantee, which "is preserved by law and sanctified by the same" (D&C 88:34). One can abide the law only as one can abide the light.

An unconditional imperative can be derived from this: Seek the increase of Christ's light. And all commandments are instrumental to this end, which is an intrinsic value. If it is said (as it is fashionable to say) that such an imperative is only binding upon me if I make it so, that if I find it unappealing, or meaningless, or even absurd, then it is not mine, and therefore not binding at all—one reply is that a measure of light itself is essential even to such a denial of the light. Christ is the true light that is in us, even when we turn our backs on him. He himself became God by abiding in the light. And even God is bound by the law.

Light as Beauty

From the understanding that light is the root of reality, of truth, and of goodness, the next step is to recognize that light is the foundation of beauty. And, again, not only does light enhance the beautiful—light itself is beautiful.

The scriptures, and notably the Book of Mormon, teem with Hebraic symbols for the beautiful and the lovely, revolving around light, brightness, fire, and whiteness. Thus of the vision of the tree of life that Lehi and Nephi beheld, it is written:

The beauty thereof was far beyond, yea, exceeding of all beauty, and the whiteness thereof did exceed the whiteness of the driven snow. (1 Nephi 11:8.)

Similarly one can feel the ancient writers straining for superlatives in their descriptions of white fruit, "above all that is white," of white robes or clothing, "nothing on earth so white," and of the white virgin, "exceeding fair and white . . . most beautiful above all virgins" (1 Nephi 11:13).

Artists have often depicted this recognition of light as divine beauty by the halo, the nimbus, and the golden circle above the head. But that is at best a token of the promise and the actuality. For "whole bodies" are promised illumination, and the light not only hovers over, but surrounds and engulfs the entire personality until it is gloriously beautiful. It was, after all, every one of the multitude, and all of each of them, even the seams of their clothing, that became scintillant with white light in the presence of Christ during that "ineffable outpouring of prayer," as Elder James E. Talmage calls it, in the 3 Nephi narrative. Modern men and women of God who have witnessed such radiance of soul say it is "like a search light turned on within." It is "the same glorious spirit," the Prophet once wrote after a vision of the resurrection, "that gives us the likeness of glory and bloom. . . . No man can describe it to you—no man can write it" (*Teachings*, p. 368). Aesthetic delight, then, whatever else it is, is delight in light. And it is surely significant that the whole color spectrum, every vivid color of the rainbow, harmonizes in white light which, in turn, harmonizes in Christ.

At the everyday level there are the light-variations in the human face, almost infinitely intimate and animate. "You will always discover, in the first glance of a man, in the outlines of his features, something of his mind," wrote the Prophet Joseph (*Teachings*, p. 299). Particularly around the eyes ("the light of the body is the eye" [Matt. 6:22]), the forehead, and the lips one sees the record as also the presence of light. It has nothing to do with fairness of complexion, with age, with cosmetic skill, with habitual patterns of facial set or mood, or even with the features we are accustomed to identify as "attractive." One must remember Isaiah's telling, should we say warning, prophecy of the Messiah—"with no apparent beauty that man should him desire" (Isaiah 53:2). Later Christ could see through the rough and rugged exterior of John the Baptist and call him "a light and burning fire." And John the Beloved could say of Christ that "in him was no darkness at all." The true beauty "in the eye of the beholder" is also in the eye of beholden, and the glory of both. It is the divine light of beauty as also the beauty of divine enlightenment, and it comes from above before it comes from within. Not all who are handsome or beautiful in the conventional sense are illumined. But all who are illumined, though conventionally "plain" or even "ugly," are beautiful.

The face may also reflect darkness. It is no abuse of terms to say that in some faces, and in all of ours at times, there is an "aura of darkness" that is disagreeable and unbeautiful, encircling in its gloom. *Darkness* here is not just a metaphor for attitude. It is an apparent absence of light that prefers and reflects "works of darkness" and finds the presence of light too much. No artifice successfully conceals it, not even a perpetual and mannerly smile. Seeking to become appealing, which is the ultimate testimony that light is good and beautiful, the adversary himself "transformeth himself nigh unto an angel of light" (2 Nephi 9:9). But his is "dark light"; and as the Master warned us, "If the light in you be darkness how great that darkness is." Having fallen from a condition of brilliant light, having flouted the inner light, Satan and those he seals his end in "outer darkness," are in deliberate darkness that cleaves to and surrounds them like a self-imposed cloak.

Light as Life

In man, the true, the good, the beautiful are not only reflected but come to life. And again the scriptures teach of the inseparable connection in fact, the eventual union in their highest forms—of light and life. "I am the light and the life of men," says the Christ. And it is his light that "giveth life to all things," that "maketh alive all things." And in man the inclusive *all* refers to the life of the mind and all the creative and responsive forces that are interwoven in him. A modern revelation speaks not only of the classic symbol "eternal life," but of "eternal lives" (D&C 132:22-25), the plural emphasizing expansion and intensification of the lives within the whole man.

As the flourishing of plant life depends upon the light-nourishment traceable to the sun in the process of photosynthesis, so the light of the sun depends upon the Son of God. "He is in the sun, and the light of the sun, and the power thereof by which it was made" (D&C 88:7). In fact, one man records that the Prophet once said, "There is no light, except the Father and the Son."[5] The nourishing that leads to the flowering of the soul—the crucial need of the soul—is his and through him ours. "I am come that they might have life, and that they might have it more abundantly." Without him we could not "abound," which is to say, live, draw breath, survive. But to abound is to abide in him and to abide in him, as vine to root, is to live abundantly.

When we are instrumental in transmitting this life-renewing power, we can be so drained that, like the Master or his modern prophets, our very "virtue" goes out and we are left visibly pale. "I became weak," said the Prophet after blessing nineteen children, "from which I have not yet recovered" (*DHC* 5:303; *Teachings,* p. 281). But when we are recipients of this power, it is the very "renewing of our bodies," the reversal of all forms of distress, disease, disability, and degeneration, and the rekindling of our emotional life. In such times the effect in us is not only the opposite of darkness; it is the opposite of heaviness or burdensome. It is the essence of spiritual and physical buoyancy. "My burden is light."

In contrast, the soul-shrinking that occurs in the absence or withdrawal of light inevitably has to do with the

---

[5]Alfred Douglas Young diary, p. 5, in Church Historian's Office.

heart's definition of life: love, and with love, joy and peace. It was John who recognized, as have few in history, that to hate is to be in darkness, and that conversely to love is to walk in the light (1 John 2:10-11). "Your minds in times past have been darkened," says a modern revelation, "because of . . . vanity and unbelief" (D&C 84:54-55). And vanity and unbelief are both ways of cutting ourselves from love, even from enlightened love of ourselves. The resulting condemnation is diminution of light, which blinds and numbs our capacities for the calm excitement of inspired love, the relish of joy, and the serenity of inner peace. We become, as Nephi told his brothers, "past feeling" and "the love of the Father does not continue with you" (D&C 95:12). This, as the scripture earlier says, is the equivalent of "walking in darkness at noonday" (D&C 95:6), or, more technically, walking in noonday light, but afflicted with a darkness "that comprehendeth it not." We literally die a little.

. . . Even Temples

We began by saying that the universe is a combination of matter and of light or spirit, and that man himself is a microscopic universe. The Lord applies to us a more majestic word: *Temples* (D&C 93:35). By divine design the temple is a microscopic man and man is a temple all alive. Standing on Mt. Scopus, northeast of Jerusalem recently, I was swept into a montage of images of temples—of Solomon, of Herod, of modern Kirtland and Nauvoo. I saw them built by the song of worthy sacrifice, endowed with encircling light and fire, and then violently desecrated, their veils ripped and trampled. Just so man, the living temple of God, can be a harmony of radiance or a divided shambles of darkness. In his vision of the future inhabitants of the holy city, John wrote:

> And I saw no temple therein; for the Lord God Almighty and the Lamb are the temple of it.

And the city had no need of the sun, neither of the moon to shine in it; for the glory of God did lighten it, and the Lamb is the light thereof.

... for the Lord God giveth them light; and they shall reign forever and ever. (Revelation 21:22-23; 22:5.)

To be light-magnified and light-purified is to have a foretaste of that temple of celestial personality: to begin to see as we are now seen by him, and to know as we are now known by him. And to enter that temple is to see God, the God of lights born in us, the lightened god or goddess that is us. And as the temple is the fusion of all of heaven and earth, so within us the real, the true, the good, and the beautiful are to be blended in the prism of perfected personality. In Christ and through Christ, the singular sheen of saintliness will be swallowed up in the "eternal burnings" of godliness.

Mormonism
and the
Nature of Man

Chauncey C. Riddle

CHAUNCEY C. RIDDLE is Dean of the Graduate School at Brigham Young University, where he has been a faculty member since 1952.

He has earned the reputation of master teacher during his distinguished educational career. He earned the B.S. degree in mathematics and physics at BYU, and then attained the M.A. and Ph.D. degrees in philosophy at Columbia University in the City of New York.

He has been an active member of the Church and at present is a high councilor in the Sharon Stake.

His wife is the former Bertha Janis Allred, and they are the parents of twelve children, ten of whom are living.

MORMONISM
AND THE NATURE OF MAN

Chauncey C. Riddle

The purpose of this paper is to delineate some of the factors pertinent to a monistic (literally "one thing") conception of man as contrasted with a dualistic conception. In the monistic thinking presently in vogue, man is seen as a material being wholly governed by the laws of the universe as discovered and formulated by science. Some persons grant that man has a spirit, but in their accounts of and treatment of man, the spiritual aspect is nonfunctional; such persons may appear to be dualists but are here classed as functional monists. The dualistic concept entertained in this paper posits mortal man as a spirit, which is the real person, and a body, which is the tabernacle of the spirit person. Though both the spirit and the body are of a material nature, dualism obtains because each represents a different order of matter; this difference is manifest in that the set of laws and influences governing the spirit aspect of man is different from that which governs the fleshly body. Basic to this whole discussion, of course, is the assumption that law and order govern all things in the universe, that all events are caused, and that there is a regularity or uniformity in the universe.

The thesis of this paper is that the key concepts of the gospel of Jesus Christ have consistency and significance only when one conceives of mortal man as a dualistic being, these values being lost if a monistic conception is adopted. The key concepts here discussed are the fall of Adam, free agency, spirituality, sin, the atonement of Jesus Christ, salvation, and righteousness.

The Fall

Before the Fall, Adam and Eve were in a monistic

state, we may presume, because they were subject to only
one set of laws and influences, those of God. Their whole
being was of a spiritual order, with spirit matter being the
life-substance of their bodies. In this condition the range of
their freedom was limited; they simply responded positively
to the commands of the Father.

The influence of Satan in tempting Eve and Adam in
the garden brought a new and opposing set of forces and
laws to bear. The Father granted Adam and Eve freedom
in the garden in that he allowed the influence of Satan to
work upon them. He allowed them to choose between His influence and that of Satan. Eve, having been deceived by
Satan, and Adam, choosing to follow her into mortality, the
anticipated death came upon our first parents. In this process
their bodies were rendered spiritually dead; spirit was re-
placed by blood in their veins and their spiritual bodies lost
the ability to perceive things in a spiritual order.

Fallen Adam was a paradigm of dualism in that his body
was fully of the order of what we call physical matter, subject to the laws and forces of a fallen realm, while his spirit,
though within the physical body, was yet subject to the laws
and forces of the spiritual order of the universe. The true
person, the spirit, was now set in opposition to the physical
body, since each was subject to a different set of laws and
forces. The Fall was thus a sundering of man, resulting in a
duality. This duality is the basis of both conflict and progress in the individual person.

What would the Fall mean if man were construed monistically? Under monism, death could only be physical; if
literal, the death of the body. But since physical death is
explicitly not part of the Fall, a monist must reject a literal
interpretation. When the spiritual death of the Fall is construed non-literally, it is usually seen either as a change of
place, the process of being cast out of the presence of God,
or as a change of the nature of man. Change of place (re-
moval from the Garden of Eden) did occur, but this change

does not exhaust the scriptural teaching concerning the Fall. If man's monistic nature were considered to change in the Fall, that change could only be accounted for by external forces. Under a monistic system, there is only one set of laws and forces. It follows that there could be no meaningful choice, and thus Adam could not be held responsible for his fall. If Adam is not responsible for his fall, he is likewise not responsible in any way to the opportunity of redemption. This, of course, renders the gospel meaningless.

Free Agency

Freedom is the opportunity to choose; agency is power. Man's free agency is then the freedom to choose and the power to attain what is chosen. Whereas God is completely free, man is but infinitesimally free; but man is free enough to respond to the influence of God, by means of which influence to become like God, or to respond to Satan and by means of that contrary influence to become like Satan.

The free agency of man, then, is limited, specific. It is a freedom given of God to the spirit in man to become free of the dominating influence of one's own physical body. It is the freedom and power to respond to the commandments of God through the Holy Spirit, thus bringing the flesh into subjection by overcoming the power and influence of Satan, which operates through the flesh. As father Lehi put it, the agency of man is to be "free according to the flesh." When that freedom is full and final, the body of man functions only under the powers, forces, and influences of the spiritual order of existence. This is to say that Satan never again has power over that being. He is free forever.

If man is construed monistically, freedom from the flesh makes no sense, for this man is only flesh. On the monistic view, if man feels free, it is either a psychological illusion or simply a physical freedom of a physical body to act without external restraint. Under monism, self-discipline is meaningless, for all discipline is a thing that must be

superimposed upon a person by outside force. Monistic freedom is the absence of that dualistic freedom, discipline of the
body by the spirit, which the gospel affords.

Spirituality

In the gospel, spirituality is the condition of the
spirit of a person being responsive to the commandments
and influences of God, specifically the influence of the Holy
Spirit. Spirituality is manifest in the control of the flesh
wherein the walking, talking, eating, drinking, working, etc.,
of a person are models of fulfilling the words of the prophets
of God to the degree to which the person is spiritual. The
more spiritual a person is, the more complete and absolute
will be the discipline of the spirit over the body.

It should not be supposed that spirituality enjoins what
is often called "asceticism." While self-denial is a frequent
choice of a spiritual person, pleasure of itself is not considered an evil. But pleasure is not sought for its own sake. A
spiritual person seeks first the kingdom of God and then to
establish in the earth the righteousness of God. In line of duty
of serving God and blessing his fellowmen, the spiritual person will strive for health, cleanliness, comeliness, strength, and
skill. But these are sought as means, not as ends. They are
means by which to glorify God and to build his kingdom,
and are an integral part of the control of the appetites and
proclivities of the physical tabernacle of the spirit. Furthermore, this control, when sought for the glory of God, re-
dounds to the blessing of the person spiritually and tempo-
rally. One of the blessings will be pleasure that is pure, un-
mixed with lust, because it is allowed rather than directly
sought. Pleasure that is spiritually pure does not turn to
pain, regret, and remorse of conscience as do pleasures sought
to gratify the appetites of the flesh.

Especially noteworthy is that the more spiritual a person
becomes, the less he will depend upon physical evidence
(through the flesh) as to what he believes. This does not

mean he ignores physical evidence; he accepts the responsibility of accounting for it, but he believes and interprets all things as he is instructed by the Holy Spirit. He will not judge on the basis of appearance.

Under a monistic system, spirituality must be classed with insanity. Since the bodies of men are demonstrably very similar, any person who does not respond "normally" to physical stimulus must be tagged as "abnormal"—insane. The more spiritual one is, the more suspect he would become to persons espousing the monistic view. Persons with great self-control cause those without it to wonder and to feel uncomfortable. To sin a little, to laugh at the possibility of perfection, to justify pleasure sought for its own sake are normal to the monist. Youth, strength, and worldly learning are honored above all else in monistic thinking because they represent the fullest accommodation and power in the realm of the physical, the realm of the flesh.

The monist also takes a curious stance of omniscience. He will not pretend in theory to know all things, but will assert that he does know all the factors pertinent to a given social problem and can therefore prescribe its solution. Thus he reserves to himself a practicing omniscience. Having denied the existence and influence of God, as a naturalist, he finds it necessary to pronounce himself at least a demi-god in order to justify rationally his practical decisions; or his intellectual systems and heroes become his demi-god. Judging by appearance and arrogating to himself sufficiency, the monist has left a trail of blood, slavery, and failure, confronted only occasionally by a John the Baptist or a Socrates who points out that he does not really know what he is doing. But the monist has ways of dealing with John and with Socrates.

To a monist, spiritual people are indistinguishable from spiritualists—those possessed of evil spirits; both are classed as insane because they do not act "normally." History shows that what is "normal" changes from age to age. There are vogues as to what is socially acceptable, fostering first one species and degree of carnality, then another. But the gospel is the same in every age: dominion of spirit over body through the gifts of God through Jesus Christ.

Sin

Sin in the gospel is breaking a commandment of God; it is acting to yield to the influence of the world upon the flesh rather than responding to the influence of God upon the spirit. Faith is willing obedience to God's Holy Spirit, and whatsoever is not of faith is sin. Sin is the triumph of the flesh over the spirit, and is therefore the triumph of Satan over the person.

In a monistic system there is no meaningful concept of sin. People are said to act strictly according to their heredity and environment, and are not to be blamed for any act, since they are not free. To change people's actions means simply to change the influences that touch them. Monists say that it is institutions of society that control men's actions. This is why control of educational programs and information media are crucial to the monist—though he never can quite account for how the governor of the system can himself escape what he is trying to cure in those whom he "benevolently" controls. The monist does not fathom the concept of repentance, because it, too, has no gospel meaning in his thought. He will look upon sex sin as "normal" and excuse any offender as if it were a light thing. Should he be a church worker, he may see social control (socialism) as the ultimate panacea, and think that in promoting social control he is doing God a favor.

The Atonement

The atonement of Jesus Christ is the central and crowning concept of the gospel. In living a perfect life as a dual being, Christ overcame the power of Satan. His life was the great triumph of spirit over flesh, the example and pattern for all mankind. In his death, the Savior climaxed that triumph by seizing from Satan the keys of death.

Through his suffering in taking the bitter cup, the Savior satisfied the demands of justice, making possible for all men an eternity free from the consequences of sin. Through his sacrifice of his life, the Savior made it possible for all men to be raised again in the resurrection with a spiritual physical body, thereafter to serve God through the spirit in eternity. As in Adam man became dual and fallen, even so in Christ men may be made spiritual and whole again, redeemed to the spiritual order of existence of their own choice.

In a monistic system, the atonement of Christ can only by the suffering and death of just another person, having efficacy for us only as it might affect us in a physical way. A monist would see the atonement at best as a symbol, as a noteworthy deed, as an ultimate protest. But he will see no connection between the shedding of the Savior's blood and the forgiveness of our sins, since the physical world affords no such causal connections; in fact, he is likely to be appalled by this idea and see it as a barbaric superstition. Thus it is possible that one who in the relative innocence of youth was cleansed and forgiven through the blood of Christ might later in his state of monistic "erudition' shed the blood of Christ afresh and put him to an open shame, not being able then to see any point in the atonement.

Salvation

Salvation in the gospel is to come to be beyond the power of one's enemies. It is a thing of degree, progressing step by step as the spirit of a person triumphs over his own flesh through faith in Jesus Christ. Considered in the aspect of being able to stop sinning, salvation is self-denial of the lusts of the flesh, and the ultimate demonstration of it is in voluntarily giving up the life of the body. Only in our death is salvation fully manifest and only in willingness to die is it fully attainable. To be free of the control of the flesh, through faith in Christ and through death, is to be forever free from Satan. If through the Savior we also gain a remission of the sins we have committed, we can then go on to inherit all that Christ has.

But salvation for the monist is quite opposite. It is ease, opulence, pleasure, comfort, and security for the flesh. The greatest of all evils for the monist is pain, though pain is challenged for that position by death. The body is the object of concern, the thing to pamper and perpetuate. Sacrifice of things material is a great misfortune. Indeed, the monist often conceives it the moral obligation of the man who has physical salvation to furnish it to others who do not; thus the monist tends to choose coercive redistributive legislation over freedom of choice and conscience. He does not even comprehend the voluntary charity of a free agent, since he cannot comprehend either charity or agency in the gospel sense.

Righteousness

In the gospel, righteousness is the way a man acts toward his neighbor when he has overcome the flesh through Christ. It is the power and authority of a saved being to bless others in leading them to Christ. A righteous man is concerned about both the physical and the spiritual needs of his fellowmen, but has no illusion that the physical needs are greater. He has kept the great law, and loves the Savior with all his heart, might, mind, and strength. And because he has kept the commandments of Christ, he is able then to love his fellowmen with the same pure love that he receives from the Savior. His goal is to make a heaven on earth where all who want to be saved can be saved, where Christ and his pure love reign supreme, where spirit has triumphed over the flesh. This involves concern for the temporal, for the material circumstances of men, as well as the spiritual. But the spiritual aspect of things is always seen as the key to progress in the material realm.

For the monist, righteousness has little meaning because sin has little meaning. To the monist, righteousness could be but conformity to human norms. The problem which the monist ever pursues is how to make a society of pleasure-seeking people productive enough to give each person all the fleshly freedom and pleasure he wants. Since that goal has never been attained (and obviously, to a dualist, cannot be attained) the substitute is slavery. With slavery, at least some can enjoy fleshly freedom and pleasure even if others have to suffer. Thus the long series of social arrangements to perpetuate control of one person by another; clergy over lay, nobles over commoners, powerful over weak, educated over uneducated, majority over minority, voters over taxpayers, caste systems, party members over nonparty members, etc. —all are bolstered by religious or moralizing theories, and all anti-Christ.

Now the real question of the whole matter is simply this: Is the universe monistic or dualistic? If the universe is monistic, then all the attendant ideas so abhorrent to the dualist are true, and the dualist is indeed insane. But if the universe is dualistic, if there is a real Savior Jesus Christ in opposition to and opposed by a real Satan, then man is a dual being, spirit opposed to flesh, and the monist is indeed in sin.

The answer would seem to lie within the individual. Does he acknowledge the voice of conscience which warns him not to yield to the lusts of the flesh? Has he sought for the influence of God through humble prayer? Has he experimented with the word of God to see if the promises are fulfilled? The testimony of the prophets is plain. They teach us of God. They teach us of dualism. They teach us to experiment honestly with our own conscience, to observe the fruits of doing the best which we know. It would seem that only the honest in heart can acknowledge the things of God, and that only those who hunger and thirst after righteousness can fully find the means by which to come unto God.

The whole purpose of life is to bring under subjection the animal passions, proclivities, and tendencies, that we might realize the companionship always of God's Holy Spirit.

—David O. McKay

A Literary Critic
Looks at the
Book of Mormon

Robert K. Thomas

ROBERT K. THOMAS is academic vice-president of Brigham Young University and past chairman of the Honors Program for gifted students.

He received his B.A. degree from Reed College in Portland, Oregon, where he was an honors scholar. He obtained the M.A. degree at the University of Oregon, and then completed his Ph.D. work at Columbia University in the City of New York.

Dr. Thomas taught first at the University of Oregon, and then joined BYU in 1951. His photographic mind and forceful method of expression never fail to challenge students to the brink of their capabilities.

He has won many academic honors, and holds membership in several professional and scholastic societies.

Active in the Church, he presently serves as a counselor in the BYU 8th Stake presidency.

He collaborated for several years with Dr. Bruce B. Clark in the compilation of cultural refinement books for the Relief Society under the title *Out of the Best Books*.

His wife is the former Shirley Wilkes, and they have three children.

A LITERARY CRITIC LOOKS
AT THE BOOK OF MORMON

Robert K. Thomas

All who read the touching lament of Jeremiah must be struck by the loneliness that is inherent in the calling of a prophet. Yet one can well imagine that he who walks with God may need no other companion. The prophet must know that most will reject him, but what protection does he have against his followers—those whose zeal to defend him is only matched by the questionable nature of their plea? Joseph Smith has fared reasonably well at the hands of his enemies, but many who revere him have almost succeeded where his enemies have failed. They speak so glibly of the Prophet Joseph as an instrument in God's hand that they have turned him into a symbol. In viewing him devotedly they try to make everything they hear about him fit. Uncritically accepting rumor with fact, conjecture with reality, they put together a pastiche which has superficial consistency but which may well be profoundly misleading. Perhaps the most embarrassing aspect of such a view is its inherent suggestion that Joseph Smith *must* be defended, and defended on the world's terms.

Many of the theories which have attempted to account for one or another of the Prophet's statements or actions reflect more faith in esoteric logic than they do in faith itself. In no area of Church scholarship has this been more evident than in the attempts which have been made to account for the manner in which the Book of Mormon was translated. While anti-Church writers—almost to a man—comment on this, no arguments have been more vehement than those which raged in our own *Improvement Era* during the first decade of this century. Advocates of the so-called

automatic theory—that is, the Urim and Thummim were
the actual translators with Joseph just a transcriber—con-
tested with proponents of the manual theory, which took its
name from the MIA manual in which it first appeared. In
this theory Joseph is viewed as the responsible translator with
the Urim and Thummim as accessories. Suffice it to say no
more was actually accomplished in this exchange than we
might expect in the light of the Book of Mormon assertion
that contention is never an appropriate avenue toward truth.

The extent to which a translator is responsible for the
diction and syntax he uses is always open to debate. The
special circumstances under which the Book of Mormon was
brought forth complicate assessing Joseph Smith's responsibility for the language and style of this work beyond useful conjecture. To say this, however, is not to say that literary criticism of the Book of Mormon is pointless. As B. H.
Roberts early asserted, the Book of Mormon is not immune
from any kind of examination: "The fact should be recognized by the Latter-day Saints that the Book of Mormon of
necessity must submit to every test, to literary criticism as
well as every other class criticism, for our age is, above all
things, critical, and especially critical of sacred literature.
We may not hope that the Book of Mormon will escape closest
scrutiny. Neither, indeed, is it advisable that it should escape." No word count, no matter how carefully collated to
show the difference between Joseph's normal style and that
used in the Book of Mormon, is going to be significant if
what the book says is not significant. No citations concerning Joseph's lack of education can make the book more mi-
raculous than it already is if it can live up to its claims.

As an early anti-Church writer bluntly puts it, "The
question is not where Smith mined it, but is it gold?" Whatever Joseph Smith's precise relationship to the expression of
the Book of Mormon is, his name is going to be linked to this
book inextricably. No consideration of Joseph Smith as a
writer can ignore the evidence of the Book of Mormon, es-

pecially the revelations of the so-called Smaller Plates of Nephi, which are free from the additional complication of major abridgment.

For over a century critics within and without the Church have reiterated the Prophet Joseph Smith's lack of literary skill. These general assertions are usually supported by specific citations which show errors in grammar or punctuation. Occasionally such unusual locutions as "the more part" are decried, or such words as "hefted" are used to indicate the influence of typical New England forms. In terms of responsible literary criticism, this is mere carping. No work is fairly judged in listing the current preferences in grammatical form. The easy pronouncements of 19th century prescriptive grammars are essentially dead today, and so is the flowery rhetoric which is more given to facade than function. The subjectivity of literary evaluation must always be recognized, but the personal need not be whimsical. If we can bring ourselves to look freshly at a work such as the Book of Mormon, we may be surprised to find more than defensive prejudgment within the Church and inattentive generalizations out of the Church have provided for us.

Until quite recently, the few attempts to look at the Book of Mormon literarily within the Church have stressed its expressive similarities to the King James version of the Bible.[1] The Bible has epistles, psalms, and lamentations. So does the Book of Mormon. The Bible displays historical narrative and prophetic discourse. So does the Book of Mormon. This substitution of a quantitative gauge for a qualitative one only suggests desperation and inevitably gives rise to a nagging suspicion that the Book of Mormon is inferior to the Bible literarily; but if we show how similar they are, if we point out that they both have the same features, maybe no one will notice how much prettier one sister is than the other.

----

[1]For two representatives of the more recent criticism see John W. Welch, "Chiasmus in The Book of Mormon," *BYU Studies* 10:1 (Aut. 1969), pp. 69-84; and John A. Tvedtnes, "Hebraisms in the Book of Mormon: A Preliminary Survey," *BYU Studies* 11:1 (Aut. 1970), pp. 50-60.

What the Book of Mormon has not yet received is critical evaluation, a true consideration of this work on the basis
of criteria which it sets for itself. These are explicitly given
on its title page and may fairly be summed up as follows:

Essentially, the Book of Mormon claims to be Hebraic
history. This claim, it should be noted, does provide a point
of contact with the Bible, but the relationship is one of matter rather than manner. Now, lest this summation seem too
modest, it must be remembered that the phrase "Hebraic
history" is a loaded one. To begin with, ancient Israel would
have found our current theories of history incredibly naive.
Our attempts to assemble objective evidence always carry the
possibility of an overlooked fact which can destroy the most
logical formulation. The Hebraic theory of history is dev-
astatingly simple and exclusive: History is God's dealings
with his chosen people—no more, no less. For example, no
attempt is made to satisfy our scientific curiosity concerning
the process of creation in Genesis 1. Biblical geography is
cited with notorious nonchalance, and we search in vain for
a truly precise chronology throughout the entire Old Testament. To Hebraic historians, records are never ends in themselves. History enables those who hear its people-oriented
account to see themselves as part of a holy race. The *hokmah*
of the proverbs, that intensely practical wisdom that has been
distilled from experience, is the hallmark of a people whose
rule is law and whose rallying cry is obedience. With profound psychological insight, ancient Israel knew that no fal-
lible human identifies easily with perfection. That is at least
one reason why we are permitted to see Abraham frightened
and Jacob indecisive. We can identify with such qualities,
and we do, but the Hebrew historian had more in mind than
a balanced presentation.

Since we have identified ourselves with men in their
weakness, we ought to grow with them as they gain strength.
Note how often we see men like Joseph and Jacob grow to
confident maturity as they respond to the hand of God on

their shoulder. Such background is necessary if we would appreciate the claims of the Book of Mormon. Details may vary, but the Hebraic pattern or manner should remain constant.

Consider, for example Nephi's account of himself in 1 Nephi. He is obviously a fine boy, but he shares the immaturity of young Joseph, young David. He is not particularly tactful with his brothers, and one contribution of his account is that he lets us see it in typically Hebraic fashion. In chapter two of 1 Nephi he states his problem very ingenuously: "I Nephi, being exceeding young, nevertheless being large in stature." His youth is still evident when he accompanies his brothers to get the plates and finally takes over the leadership of the little expedition. Coming upon Laban drunken, he appears to be less overwhelmed by the evident opportunity to get the plates than he is by that beautiful sword, and when the Spirit tells him he must kill Laban, he is shocked. The Spirit has to urge him once more, at which point he begins a halfhearted, high school rationalization which is climaxed by the lame assertion that, after all, Laban has stolen their property. Only after the Spirit commands him the third time does he begin to see the relationship of the precepts he has so dutifully memorized to the realities of this moment. He has started to grow up. Fulfilling the commandment and donning the clothes of Laban—remember that "large in stature"—he tries to make his voice deep like Laban's and, picking up Zoram, heads for the treasury.

In his growing excitement, as he actually touches the sacred records, he undergoes an all-to-human lapse. He tells Zoram that he will carry the records to his "elder brethren who were without the walls." With what terror young Nephi must have heard himself say this in his anxiety. Laban had no brothers outside of the walls. With what a pounding heart he must have bade the servant follow him. What a breath of relief there is in the following verse: "And he, supposing that I spake of the brethren of the church, and I was truly that Laban whom I had slain, wherefore he did follow me."

As they contact Nephi's brothers, Zoram is suddenly aware of the whole deception and turns to flee. Whereupon Nephi seizes him and in so doing describes himself in the following significant phrase: "And now I, Nephi, being a man." He has matured overnight. The sobering awareness of what serving the Lord may entail has been a refining fire. Note particularly from this time on his understanding attempts to help his brothers. No longer is he merely exhorting them to righteousness. He tries everything to help them. Also note how tactfully and lovingly he takes over for his father when Lehi finally breaks under the continuing strain of providing food for his family in the wilderness. The story of Jacob's wrestle with the angel is not so dramatically related. How skillfully we see Nephi develop. This is Hebraic history of a high order. Biblical analogues to this story are all inferior to it in focus and in illuminating detail.

One exquisitely appropriate story does not, of course, justify the book. But his becomes an *experimentum crucis*, that critical example which it must be accounted for. Other examples are not wanting. Consider, also, the story of Abinadi, the mildly reluctant prophet. He is careful to make it clear that his preaching is strictly at the Lord's behest, and he goes into hiding when King Noah issues orders to have him killed. When he returns, two years later—for he is a dutiful man and he knows he should go back—he reappears in disguise. But what are his opening words? "Thus has the Lord commanded me, saying—Abinadi. . . ." What use is a false mustache when he has just identified himself? You could worry a little about Abinadi at this point. The priests evidently are contemptuous of him and prepare to catch him in his words so they can execute him. But something happens to Abinadi when he realizes he is going to have to die for what he believes. No one is going to listen to him; they are going to kill him. And suddenly he too grows up. Any reluctance which seemed to hedge his efforts to begin with is burned away. It is a tremendous story. Another favorite of mine is the account of Korihor, the fellow traveler, the Communist. Read Alma 30 again with its skillful propounding of dialectical materialism. How hard it is to control a man who does not carry any dynamite himself but who advocates blowing up the city hall. Is that an overt action? Then, as now, the people were puzzled and frustrated.

I suggest that these are but a few of many stories that are arresting in themselves, but also clearly in the Hebraic tradition. Their only defect is a shared one. Since they occur in those parts of the book which have been abridged, they lack the spontaneity of 1 Nephi.

Incidental but very interesting evidence concerning the possible age of the language from which Joseph Smith is translating occurs when we come across a word like "ziff" in Mosiah 11:3. Together with "neas and sheum" of Mosiah 9:9 and "cureloms and cumoms" of Ether 9:19, we have some very convincing examples of what are technically known as *hapax legomena*. Linguistically, such terms are a part of almost all ancient records. Indeed they become a check on their age. *Hapax legomena* are terms which cannot be translated, only transliterated—that is, put into the sounds of a language. Epics such as Beowolf, an ancient Anglo-Saxon epic poem, display them often, as does the Bible in a term like *selah*. No one knows what *selah* means. As a child I thought it must mean "Amen," because it came at the end of things. Now our best guess is that it is a musical notation because it is only found in Biblical lyrics.

Similarly the examples cited from the Book of Mormon are still unknown. Since the significance of *hapax legomena* in establishing the authenticity of ancient records is a relatively recent development, actually given most of its impetus by Germanic higher criticism of the last part of the 19th century, their occurrence in the Book of Mormon is persuasive internal evidence of its claims.

But perhaps the most remarkable demonstration of literary sensitivity in the entire Book of Mormon can be enjoyed in the seven pages which comprise the books of Enos, Jarom, and Omni. Though these books at first glance seem too short to be very significant, they are actually a tour de force without parallel in Hebraic scripture, illustrating that style is the man.

The headlong impetuosity of Enos is suggested by his rather imprecise, fragmentary opening sentence. As an English teacher this always makes me shiver a little as I read it. "Behold, it came to pass that I, Enos, knowing my father that he was a just man—for he taught me in his language, and also in the nurture and admonition of the Lord—and blessed be the name of my God for it."

The vitality of this man fairly crackles on the page. Note especially his use of verbs and verb forms; "wrestled, sunk, hungered, kneeled, cried, raised, poured out, struggling, swept." Enos simply cannot wait for logic to catch up with him. His words roll forth in an irresistible flood. In describing the Lamanites he pours attitudes on top of environment, adds physical description, then skills, shifts to diet and back to attitudes again. His sentences all have a spoken quality, and their lengths seem determined only by a need for breath. Listen as you read the following description of his own people: "And there was nothing save it was exceeding harshness, preaching and prophesying of wars, and contentions, and destructions, and continually reminding them of death, and the duration of eternity, and the judgments and the power of God, and all these things—stirring them up continually to keep them in the fear of the Lord." Just one magnificent sentence—about a deep breath long!

This man wrings meaning from every moment. His concluding words are beautifully in character: "And I rejoice in the day when my mortal shall put on immortality, and shall stand before him; then shall I see his face with pleasure." It has been suggested that in all Western literature there is a singular lack of friendship toward God. Reverence, awe, wonder, transport, even ecstacy we know; but all these have overtures of the supernal. Enos, in the company of the the English poet George Herbert, might well make an affectionate call on the Lord.

From Enos to his son Jarom is the shortest of genealogical steps but a gigantic shift in style. Except for the expected, conventional beginning, note the difference: "Now behold, I, Jarom, write a few words according to the commandment of my father, Enos, that our genealogy may be kept." You are suddenly aware that nothing in the whole Book of Enos came to bear on a problem with such crispness. The succeeding verses develop the reasons for the length of his account and the special problems of his day in coherent, beautifully modulated sentences. His diction too is precise. In discussing his people he lets us see their total strength in saying that "They profaned not, neither did they blaspheme." This is not merely synonymous parallelism, that standard device of Hebraic poetry; this is an incremental repetition in which additional meanings are added within a parallel framework.

Too many readers of the Book of Mormon have failed to appreciate its quality by setting their own limited understanding as the gauge of excellence. *Profane* (literally "before the temple") suggests general irreverence, most commonly heard in light-minded reference to holy things. As serious as this is, it does not connote the deliberate defiance which is suggested by blasphemy. Thoughtless people may profane; the intentionally wicked blaspheme.

Note how carefully the general denunciations of Enos are focused in Jarom. In verse 20 Enos describes the Lamanites as being of "such evil nature they became wild and ferocious, a bloodthirsty people, full of idolatry and filthiness." Jarom's accusation is precise: "They loved murder. . . ." Perhaps more clearly than we have understood before we here see the hopelessness of the Lamanite attitude, with its calculated wickedness.

The remainder of Jarom's account is similarly discriminating. In verse 11 he comments that it was possible to teach the law of Moses but the people had to be persuaded to look forward to the Messiah. Once more this is just the right distinction. The law of Moses was not only a fact of holy writ, it was a fact of experience. It could be rationally apprehended. The concept of a Messiah on the other hand was in the realm of things yet to come; it required emotional reinforcement, which is just the connotation sounded by "persuaded."

From calm, exacting Jarom we come to Omni. At once we are struck by a focus on the first person. There are seven "I"s in two verses. Omni is a soldier, dutifully carrying out the command of his father but not a bit averse to identifying himself as a wicked man. We soon see what really interests him. He not only lets us know of his valor in battle but describes his times solely in terms of war and peace. "We had many seasons of peace, and we had many seasons of serious war and bloodshed."

That reference to "serious war" gives him away. It suggests the concern of a man for whom war is neither inconsequential nor detestable. It is simply a vocation. Omni is forthright, not very reflective, and his sentences march briskly but to no great end.

Amaron, Omni's son, is more like his grandfather, Jarom. He is careful, organized, and in a few verses manages to turn our attention from personalities to issues. Yet Amaron lacks Jarom's linguistic sensitivity. His sentences, unlike Omni's, are neatly balanced, but it is a mechanical neatness. Here is a style which tries to synthesize the no-nonsense approach of his father with the carefully controlled cadence of his grandfather.

If Amaron is not quite successful, what shall we say of Chemish? Poor, dear Chemish! Possibly he did not expect to have to take his turn at the records, since they usually went from father to son, but overwhelmed by the responsibility that is suddenly his, he can only belabor the obvious: "They all write in the same book, and they all write with their own hands." You can just see the half-hopeful, half-relieved smile with which he turns the records over to his son.

I know of no more revealing verse in all scripture. How clearly Chemish is given to us. Not in what is said about him, but in what he says about himself through his style. Just one verse, but in it the whole history of inadequacy. The ghosts of my own failures clamor for recognition from my sub-conscious whenever I hear the name Chemish. I am related to him by all the blundered opportunity, the embarrassed incompetence that has threaded itself through my own life.

It is a relief to pass on to Abinadom. But in reading his account I seem to detect a bit of insecurity. I suspect he has looked back to see what others have written. There are echoes of Omni and Jarom, but nothing else. At this point we have had four men write in a total of eleven verses. This is all we know of them, yet I feel I might recognize them on the street.

The final nineteen, rather long verses are the breezy contribution of Amaleki. He just loves to write. He mixes exhortation and history in about equal amounts and stops only when he has used up all the space that remained on the plates.

Joseph Smith's translation of the small plates concludes here. Not only have we encountered typically Hebraic fig-ures, but they have been presented with undeniable skill. Styles which should have been distinctive have been con-sistently so. Yet there is an overall tone which bespeaks a single translator.

We have only to check the markedly different versions of the Bible in English to recognize how much a translator can provide in achieving that integration of nuance and emphasis that turns words into life. It is a temptation which space really will not allow to comment on the many small but significant changes which the Book of Mormon details in the celebrated words of Isaiah. Critics here have ignored the discriminating differences. Equally worthy of comment are the beautiful extensions given the Savior's words in 3 Nephi. One in particular I find so full of insight that in it alone I begin to recognize some of the plain and precious truths which unending translations have taken from the Bible.

In the Sermon on the Mount in Matthew 5:6-7, there is an injunction to avoid becoming angry with your brother without a cause, lest you be brought to the judgment. Now I have never been angry in my life without a cause. Someone or something has always made me angry. The Book of Mormon allows me no such rationalization: "But I say unto you, whosoever is angry with his brother shall be in danger of his judgment."

How profoundly this extends the Biblical idea. In leaving out "without a cause" I am blocked from shifting the responsibility for my own lack of control, and in substituting "his judgment" for "the judgment," I see my anger against my brother starting a train of judgment and counter judgment which leads inevitably to the more serious consequences elaborated upon in the rest of this verse.

Can anyone seriously question the inspired nature of translations such as the one just cited? Yet to say that Joseph Smith was inspired is not really to say enough. In some sense all good writing is inspired. The traditional invoking of the Muse is only a formalized recognition of a basic need to draw on some power which can breathe life into the feelings and ideas to which we would give expression. The inspiration that attends the translation of sacred records, however, must be a very special kind, in the nature of a gift and partaking of the power of God.

In one of the few comments which we have from the Lord concerning sacred translation, he suggests the person who is entrusted with his gift must study out in his mind the material under consideration and then ask him whether or not it is correct. If it is, the Lord will cause the translator's bosom to burn with the knowledge that what he is writing has divine sanction. How the Prophet Joseph's bosom must have burned as he was translating the Book of Mormon! We shall never learn to appreciate this book fully until we too prepare a temple for the flame.

Centrifugal
Tendencies in
Mormon History

Leonard J. Arrington

LEONARD J. ARRINGTON, for many years professor of economics at Utah State University, has just been appointed Church Historian, and director of the Redd Center of Western Studies at Brigham Young University.

These significant recent appointments come after a long and illustrious career of writing, teaching, and Church service.

Dr. Arrington graduated from the University of Idaho and received the Ph.D. degree in economics from the University of North Carolina. He has taught in North Carolina, and at USU since 1946, in addition to other assignments at the University of California, BYU, and the University of Genoa, Italy.

He has written numerous books, articles, and pamphlets especially for professional economic and historical publications.

In the Church he has served as teacher, high councilor, and member of a stake presidency.

He and his wife, the former Grace Fort, have three children.

CENTRIFUGAL TENDENCIES
IN MORMON HISTORY

Leonard J. Arrington

The spectacular growth of The Church of Jesus Christ of Latter-day Saints in the first two decades after its founding in 1830 insured that it would attract a variety of converts, not all of whom were converted for the same reasons or had the same understanding of the Church's beliefs and practices. Quite obviously, in a movement of this size, there were converts who were attracted by certain aspects of the Restoration and were repelled by others. Some of these early convert-members became so preoccupied with certain doctrines and customs, either through positive attraction or negative repulsion, that they rode their particular hobbies and predispositions right out of the Church. The intellectual and personal qualities of some of these apostates permitted them to attain distinction in other cultures and movements. In this way the centrifugal tendencies of Mormonism threw out an occasional individual who carried with him some of the beliefs and attitudes he had acquired as a Latter-day Saint.

In this essay I shall discuss some of the aberrations that led to individual apostasy and describe briefly the experiences of six persons who left the Church in the nineteenth century because of the aberrations. The particular six were chosen because they left books, speeches, or diaries that articulate the attitudes and activities that led to their apostasy and/or excommunication. These men provide a focus for viewing tendencies that attracted or repelled early Church members, divided and polarized the membership of the Church, and produced in a few notorious instances widely-circulated books of repudiation.

The first of the aberrations involved a misunderstanding of the role of Joseph Smith. Moving from acceptance of Joseph Smith as a prophet, seer, and revelator, some members proceeded to deify him. If the Lord would condescend to speak to Joseph when he had failed to speak to so many for so long, surely this prophet must be the greatest person who ever lived! When some of those who had made Joseph virtually divine discovered, upon further experience, that he was quite human, that he made mistakes, and that he had observable imperfection and deficiencies, they promptly classified him as a fraud. Disappointed and bitter at these discoveries, they struck out, loudly proclaiming his shortcomings and vindictively seeking to expose the falsity of his pretensions.

The first notable case of this was Ezra Booth, a former Methodist minister who had converted in 1831. After remaining a member for only five months, he apostatized and wrote nine letters that were published in the Ravenna, Ohio, *Star*. As summarized by Max Parkin, these letters asserted the inconsistencies in the Prophet's revelations, the despotic tendencies of Joseph Smith and his fellow leaders, and the manifest weaknesses in the characters and personalities of Joseph Smith and his associates. In regard to the latter, Booth criticized the Prophet for "a want of sobriety, prudence, and stability" and for possessing "a spirit of lightness and levity, a temper of mind easily irritated, and an habitual proneness to jesting and joking." In summary, Booth said that Joseph's revelations were "something short of infallible."[1]

Approximately two years after the initial publication of Booth's letters, another prominent convert, Philastus Hurlburt, with the encouragement and support of a special committee of anti-Mormons, undertook an investigation designed to expose Mormonism and humiliate its founder. The well-

[1]"Letter Number VII," *Ohio Star*, November 24, 1831, cited in Max H. Parkin, *A Study of the Nature and Causes of External and Internal Conflict of the Mormons in Ohio Between 1830 and 1838* (Provo, Utah: Department of Seminaries and Institutes of Religion, 1967), p. 84.

known result, edited and expanded by Eber M. Howe, was *Mormonism Unvailed; or, a Faithful Account of that Singular Imposition and Delusion from its Rise to the Present Time* (Painesville, Ohio, 1834). This book advanced the Spaulding-Rigdon theory of the origin of the Book of Mormon, contained a lengthy review of the contents of the Book of Mormon, related uncomplimentary incidents in the history of the Church, reproduced Booth's nine letters, and attached a large number of affidavits from former "neighbors" of the Smith family in New York and Pennsylvania that described the Smiths as ignorant, improvident, superstitious, and deceitful. Booth's letters and the Hurlburt-Howe book served to warn Church members that they must not tie Mormonism too closely to Joseph Smith. Joseph was the founding prophet, to be sure, but there would be other prophets. His translation of the Book of Mormon represented one of the cornerstones, but still just a cornerstone. And his leadership was authoritative and commanding, but only to the extent that, and only as long as, the Lord willed it so. In short, there was far more to Mormonism than Joseph Smith, and converts were reminded that Jesus was the head of the Church.

The second aberration that led to apostasy was an overemphasis of the concept of the secular kingdom of God, involving the acquisition of territory, the establishment of governments, the promotion of business, and political and financial scheming. In such a world, religion as we ordinarily understand it could become a secondary consideration—indispensable perhaps, but not all inclusive—a convenient unifying device but hardly the cynosure. Entering this temporal scene in 1840 was Dr. John C. Bennett, an aggressive and versatile developer and promoter. During the 1830's Bennett had promoted medical schools, educational institutions, masonic lodges, land projects, and state militias. And there are contemporary allegations that he promoted himself particularly well with the ladies. A successful physician, Bennett was said to have been the first man after William Morton to use ether in anesthesia. He invented an improved type of dental forceps called Bennett forceps, and published a text on gynecology and several important articles in medical journals. For a period he was a Methodist minister. Later, he joined the Campbellites and became a close friend of Alexander Campbell. He was also Quartermaster General of the Illinois State Militia. Well-educated, personable, and able, if somewhat erratic and conceited, Bennett was an organizer, idea man, and adventurer.

Clearly, the kingdom was in need of a man with Bennett's talents, and could profit from his ambitions. This is apparently what Joseph Smith saw in him, and the Prophet was at least persuaded that Bennett was sincere in hitching his career to the rising star of Mormonism.[2] Nor was the Prophet mistaken about the doctor's abilities. During the eighteen months he was in Nauvoo, General Bennett rendered yeoman service for the temporal kingdom. He secured the Nauvoo Charter; organized and trained the Nauvoo Legion, of which a promising young lieutenant, Robert E. Lee, had good things to say; founded the Nauvoo Agricultural and Manufacturing Society; and established the University of the City of Nauvoo. The desirability and effectiveness of Bennett's contributions are indicated by the fact that they were all duplicated later in Utah. Of Bennett's enthusiastic acceptance by the community there can be not doubt. He was elected mayor of Nauvoo, sustained as a member of the First Presidency of the Church, and appointed chancellor of the University of the City of Nauvoo.

But of course Mormonism was more than political conniving, splendid military parades, and the establishment of prestigious universities. There are intimations in contemporary documents that General Bennett became the ring-

---

[2]Despite Bennett's assertion that he joined the Church expressly to expose Mormon pretentions and deceits, it is difficult to believe that this could have been hidden from Joseph Smith. It seems more likely that Bennett was a believer, but with vulnerable weaknesses.

leader of a conspiracy to dump Joseph Smith and take over the military and political apparatus of the kingdom. No doubt Bennett dreamed of establishing an independent western empire. At any rate, power considerations seem to have been important to him. Not particularly concerned with theology, spirituality, or even morals, the General was bound to clash with Joseph Smith. When he was relieved of his offices and left Nauvoo, Bennett took with him an intimate knowledge of some of the confidential conversations and hopes and designs of the Church and its leaders. Urged on by apostates and anti-Mormons, he published some of these to the world, adding for good measure disclosures that were figments of his own imagination. The result was *The History of the Saints; or, An Exposé of Joe Smith and Mormonism* (Boston, 1842). It was a dull book, filled with affidavits and letters, as if he were attempting to establish a legal case against the Prophet. He also relied heavily on material previously published by Hurlburt-Howe and Thomas Sharp, editor of the anti-Mormon Warsaw *Signal*.[3]

It is interesting to find confirmation of General Bennett's enterprise and energy in his subsequent career. In Massachusetts, he promoted agricultural and manufacturing improvements; introduced the Plymouth Rock chicken, perhaps the single most important step in poultry breeding in America in the nineteenth century; and launched the first annual poultry exhibition in the United States—a show which 10,000 persons paid to see on the Boston Common. He held important positions in the Union Army during the Civil War, and ended his days as a progressive agriculturist in Polk County, Iowa. While there he wrote a text on breeding poultry which was used in agricultural colleges until recent times.

Chronologically, the third aberration was a supposed extension of the temporal kingdom concept. The mainstream

---

[3]That he joined James J. Strang in Wisconsin after Joseph Smith's assassination suggests that his quarrel may have been with Church leadership rather than the Mormon religion.

of the Church was well acquainted with the mixture of temporal and spiritual that existed in the principal Latter-day Saint gathering places in Kirtland, Missouri, and Illinois. But American members who did not gather to these central places, and members converted in Europe, had little opportunity to observe and participate in the temporal aspects of the kingdom. Their knowledge of the Church was largely limited to missionary sermons and tracts. To many of them at least the essence of Mormonism was a revolutionary view of man and God, the outpouring of spiritual gifts, and the epic of God's renewed intercession in the affairs of men.

Meanwhile the main body of the Latter-day Saints moved on to the Great Basin. Here in the valleys of the mountains, if never before, the Saints had to come to grips with the problems of physical survival. Not a lush land carpeted with grass and trees, the mountain valleys and deserts presented challenges that few American settlers had encountered. Making a living involved fighting crickets and grasshoppers, combating winds and dust, digging canals, getting timber out of the canyons, and enduring the frustrations and fears of unpredictable Indians. Since the community of Saints was virtually identical with the community of settlers, these and other practical matters were discussed in priesthood and sacrament meetings. Quite natural, one might say, but was it really proper to use priesthood and sacrament meetings to talk about building cowpens, starting tanneries, setting a guard, and managing the scarce supply of water? Latter-day Saints who remained in the Midwest, where it was still possible to have individualism in religion, politics, and economics, were inclined to look upon these temporal preoccupations as lapses from spirituality—as a form of theocracy inconsistent with American democracy and freedom. Similarly, the British Saints, reared in non-conformist traditions and skeptical of claims of infallibility, particularly in matters they regarded as peripheral to religion, did not regard these temporal concerns as essential elements in the gospel. They were, to many Britishers, a crudity, an example of frontier uncouthness, a sure neglect of spirituality. Mormonism, to them, was nothing if not spiritual.

An intelligent and classically-educated English convert who was affected by the Church's attitude toward temporalities was John Hyde. Converted in 1848 at the age of 15, he had been a missionary in England and France and came to the Salt Lake Valley in 1853 at the age of 20. He found the materialism of the Utah Saints revolting. He could not bridge the gap between his own mystical vision of God and the crude reality of the kingdom of God in the mountains. He thought the eleven-hour ceremony in the Endowment House offensive to good taste and decency, and the excesses of the 1856 reformation were even more coarse and vulgar to this sensitive and refined young Englishman. He had been converted by the remarkable pamphlets and powerful sermons of two of the Church's greatest missionaries, Orson Pratt and John Banks, both of whom tended to be somewhat visionary and philosophical, just like young Hyde. When the young immigrant's horror at the trend of things in Utah came to the attention of Brigham Young, the president sent him on a mission to Hawaii. There he would be back in his beloved mission field, in a region noted for its absence of materialism, where he would have ample opportunity to cultivate the spiritualities of his adopted faith.

John Hyde went on the mission, but his agonizing withdrawal from the community of Latter-day Saints had already progressed too far. His sermons in Hawaii, and later in San Francisco, were filled with disclosures and remarks that could only be interpreted as anti-Church. He then wrote *Mormonism, Its Leaders and Designs* (New York, 1857), a persuasive and damaging anti-Mormon book. Inasmuch as he was still only 24 years of age when the book appeared, Brother Hyde's work was inevitably affected by the emotional trauma of his disenchantment. He had made a total commitment; he had left his home country to work and struggle with the

Saints in the Great Basin. But he felt that his intellectual talents and capabilities were not appreciated, and his dreams of a pure and undefiled religion were punctured. Elder Hyde now felt a psychological necessity to explain to his friends why he had become estranged. His reason and judgment distorted by the anguish of his soul, Elder Hyde's picture of Mormonism, while in part true, was ugly and denunciatory.[4]

Returning to England after the publication of his book, John Hyde became active in the Swedenborgian movement, and wrote several books and lectures before his death in 1875 at the age of 42. They include: *Emmanual Swedenborg, The Man of the Age* (London, 1859); *Will the Natural Body Rise from the Grave?* (London, 1859); *The Story and Divinity of the Holy Bible and Its Spiritual Sense* (London, 1862); *The Serpent that Beguiled Eve* (London, 1862); *The Angels* (London, 1875); *Character: Its Elements and Development* (London, 1875); *Our Eternal Homes* (London, 1877); and *The Doctrine of Substitution Impartially Examined* (Edinburgh, 1880?). Thoughtful, sophisticated, and productive, John Hyde undeniably would have enriched our literature if the Church could have retained him.

The fourth aberration was spiritism or spiritualism—a preoccupation with phenomena, as opposed to material things, such that one is propelled into the unreal world of disincarnate spirits and demons, of ghosts and poltergeists, of mediums, ectoplasm, and automatic writing. This tendency illustrates the problem of building a testimony on action and reaction. A number of British converts reacted so strongly against Mormon materialism and priesthood infallibility in the sphere of temporalities that they embraced spiritualism. This movement in Church history is usually referred to as the Godbeite schism. The British-born Godbeites were soon joined by a spiritual-minded American, Amasa Lyman, a Latter-day Saint since 1832, an apostle since 1842, and or-

---

[4]Joseph E. Hyde, a younger brother with whom he had traveled from England to Utah, settled in Logan, Utah, and remained a valuable and devoted member of the Church.

dained by Joseph Smith to be counselor in the First Presidency shortly before the latter's assassination. Intelligent, sensitive, and one of the great preachers in the Church, Apostle Lyman became president of the Godbeite-inspired "Church of Zion" in 1870.

It is curious that Brother Lyman could become so completely enmeshed in spiritualism as to conduct hundreds of séances during the early 1870's. Not surprisingly, the messages that he presumed to receive from departed spirits were hardly more than inane banalities—singularly uninspired and uninspiring. Nevertheless the arbitrariness of priesthood rule was galling to him, and the spiritual life was real. Records show that hundreds of Latter-day Saints joined Brother Lyman in these séances. A convert to something called Harmonial Philosophy, Amasa Lyman was also a devoted reader of *Banner of Light,* a paper published by the spiritualists of Boston. Some of the many articles about Mormonism in that publication may have been written or inspired by Amasa Lyman.

A related aberration, our fifth, was the excessive emphasis upon mental health and faith healing. Our Lord, the scriptures tell us, went about healing the sick, raising the dead, causing the lame to walk, blessing the blind to receive their sight and the deaf to hear, and "curing all manner of diseases." (Mosiah 3:5) In nineteenth-century America some believers exalted this principle of mental and physical health to a position of absolute primacy, and thus produced a distorted version of the gospel. Among these faiths, as Latter-day Saints believe, was Christian Science, a faith that teaches that thought governs everything, including the body, and that sin and sickness can be eliminated by a deeper and more serene understanding of Jesus' teaching and healing.

About the same time that Amasa Lyman was embracing spiritualism, Brigham Bicknell Young, son of Joseph Young and nephew of the Prophet Brigham, had exhausted the opportunities for musical instruction in Utah and was sent by his brothers Seymour and LeGrande to England to continue his training. He enrolled in the National Training School of Music, the Royal College of Music under the patronage of the Prince of Wales, who later became Edward VII. Bicknell developed a rich baritone voice that earned him the plaudits of music connoisseurs in Italy as well as in England. After his graduation in 1883, Brother Young married Elisa Mazzucato, a native of Milan, also a teacher of music. Two years later he brought her and their first son to the United States. After five years in the West, he established himself as a teacher of voice in Chicago.

In 1890, Brother Bicknell became ill, and his family and friends despaired of his life. When he was healed through the kindness of a Christian Science practitioner, he began to study that belief and was converted. In 1901 he became an authorized teacher of Christian Science, and two years later gave up his music profession to join the Christian Science Board of Lectureship. His lectures were well received, and he was the first Christian Scientist to complete a world lecture tour. In London he lectured to 8,000 persons in the Royal Academy; among those listening was Queen Victoria herself. Brother Young's influence for good was such that upon the death of Mary Baker Eddy, this son of Mormon parents in Salt Lake City was chosen to be Mrs. Eddy's successor, becoming Reader for the Mother Church, The First Church of Christ Scientist, and in that capacity leader of Christian Scientists throughout the world. There is a considerable file of printed sermons delivered by Brother Young on behalf of the Christian Science faith, and they reveal a person of literary ability with powers of thought and expression and natural persuasiveness. Latter-day Saints have not publicized the contributions to American religion of this product of our culture, but unquestionably here is one local boy who rose to great prominence.

A sixth and final aberration of nineteenth-century Mormonism was rationalism—the overweening emphasis on science, education, and mental enlightenment. Young Latter-day Saint intellectuals were influenced, just as American intellectuals generally were influenced, by Charles Darwin, Thomas Huxley, the Higher Criticism, and what might be referred to as the new learning. Occasionally, as one might expect, a young Latter-day Saint was so impressed with the new learning that he went beyond demythologization and concluded that there was little more to religion than superstition.

One of the bright young Latter-day Saints in the late 1860's who had this problem was Theodore W. Curtis. The new learning was not consonant with his concept of Mormonism. A precocious writer, thoughtful speaker, and graduate of the University of Deseret, Brother Curtis ran a bookstore in Salt Lake City. Ultimately, he became so impressed with his books and the message he thought they conveyed, that he left the local culture and migrated to Boston. This was not an easy decision for him—he had to leave behind his wife and baby son. At the outset, he had asked very little of his family and his brethren—only that they acknowledge that one could legitimately derive inspiration from Plato and Socrates, from Dante and Shakespeare, and from Bacon and Darwin, as well as from Latter-day Saint writings and scriptures.

At any rate, Brother Curtis lost his faith in a vain attempt to package his learning in the traditional forms of the belief in which he had been reared. He went to Boston; joined with the Unitarians; wrote regularly for their paper, *The Index;* and made a living writing for newspapers and national magazines. The Unitarians, of course, were not strong on creed. They emphasized freedom of individual belief, the use of reason, religious tolerance, the brotherhood of man, and programs of social improvement. Within this liberal framework, Theodore Curtis could retain most features of the religion in which he was brought up. Further accenting his restiveness under traditional constraints to reason and freedom, Brother Curtis was among the founders of the Free

Religious Association, a dissident group of Unitarians who held out for the essential humanity of Jesus and opposed such beliefs as the virgin birth, literal resurrection, and the necessity of priesthood mediation.

Lonely but unregenerate, Brother Curtis devoted the rest of his life to writing and working for progressive causes and the rights of organized labor. He remained fond of the Mormon culture and rendered a real service to the Church during the 1880's by writing articles favorable to the Latter-day Saints in national periodicals and newspapers. Although he died in the 1930's in exile, as it were, his son in Utah became one of the truly great poets and literary figures in the Church. Not more than a decade after Theodore removed himself from the culture, Latter-day Saint teachers were making such adaptations in their presentations that hardly any young Latter-day Saint intellectuals felt constrained to make the break that Theodore Curtis had made. The next generation, under the leadership of Karl G. Maeser, James E. Talmage, N. L. Nelson, W. H. Chamberlain, and other distinguished philosophers and scientists, demonstrated the error of forcing young scholars to choose between science and religion. As they saw it, the gospel was truth, truth took many forms, and scientific truths were harmonious with religious truths.

Each of the apostasies I have described was tragedy. To lose any soul is tragic enough; to lose men of this caliber and sensitivity is doubly tragic. Apostasies force agonizing choices, create tortured feelings of guilt and anxiety, and alienate individuals from the society of their families and friends. The necessity of justifying their apostasy caused some of them—Hurlburt, Bennett, and Hyde—to write hate-filled books containing bitter epithets and diatribes, but with little explanation of the reasons they became Mormons in the first place. Nevertheless Latter-day Saint historians cannot avoid reading their books. Latter-day Saint scholars who have not wrestled with anti-Mormonism cannot really understand the potential conflicts in Mormon culture and values.

As Richard Crossman wrote, "The Devil once lived in Heaven, and those who have not met him are unlikely to recognize an angel when they see one."[5]

There is some consolation in the knowledge that the six unfaithful Mormons I have described, after becoming healed of the sores of their apostasy, made contributions to the organizations and societies they joined. The moral, spiritual, intellectual, and esthetic excellence of Mormonism can be measured not only by the enrichment of the lives of those who function exclusively within the Church, but also by the desirable qualities of mind and character that members and former members have carried and continue to carry to those outside the culture. If it is a positive force for good, as we all believe, Mormonism, in its journey through history, will flick out into the secular world and the world of other faiths, arresting and stimulating ideas, practices, and attitudes that will help mankind to advance along the path of peace and brotherhood and enhance the enjoyment of personal and group life. Unfortunately the Church has "lost" persons of genius and creativity to other religions, to business, to the professions, to literature, to the performing arts, to political activity, and to the world of sports. Hopefully our loss has been the gain of the organizations and cultures into which dissenting products of Mormon culture have been absorbed.

Whoever loses or gains, it would be well for all of us in the Church to look to our own lives, interests, and testimonies to see that we maintain a balanced life and guard against following one of these six paths to loss of faith and apostasy. If Latter-day Saint educators do their jobs properly, members and former members of this Church will carry with them qualities of mind and modes of behavior that will influence the world for good and prepare the way for the Second Coming. If this ideal holds up in practice, we can proudly boast: "Once a Mormon, always a Mormon!"

_____

[5] *The God That Failed* (New York, 1963), p. 11.

Reciprocal Loyalty: The Administrative Imperative

Martin B. Hickman

MARTIN B. HICKMAN is Dean of the College of Social Sciences, and professor of Political Science at Brigham Young University. He holds two graduate degrees from the University of Utah and one from Harvard.

A former foreign service officer for the U. S. State Department, he has distinguished himself as a teacher and administrator at the University of Southern California and BYU.

He has written widely on political and religious subjects. His latest book is *The Military and American Society* (Glencoe Press, 1971).

A former member of a bishopric, Dr. Hickman is a Sunday School teacher in the Oak Hills First Ward, Sharon East Stake. He has served also in a branch presidency in Hamburg, Germany, and in Stake YMMIA leadership positions. He also served in the French Mission, 1947-49.

He and his wife, JoAnn, are the parents of six daughters.

RECIPROCAL LOYALTY:
THE ADMINISTRATIVE IMPERATIVE

Martin B. Hickman

One of the J. Golden Kimball stories frequently retold has it that at a stake conference in central Utah, Elder Kimball, while reading the list of stake officers to be sustained, proposed that Mt. Nebo be moved fifty miles to the south. The conference congregation, so the story goes, duly gave its sustaining vote to this proposal. The implication of this story is that the sustaining process is often mechanical and without meaningful content. The thesis of this essay is that just the contrary is true—that however mechanistic the sustaining vote appears on the surface, it represents in most cases a profound commitment to the goals and leaders of the Church. The result is a deep sense of organizational loyalty which eases the task of Church administrators if they can respond to this loyalty in meaningful ways.

I

Much misunderstanding of the sustaining process by members of the Church stems from a mistaken comparison with secular elections. An election is the process of expressing a preference for one candidate over another. It may be, therefore, merely a negative act; election does not necessarily mean that the winner is the optimal choice of the electorate, but only that he is preferred over his opponent; or, put in another way, disliked less. Since the vote may therefore be a rejection of one candidate rather than approval of another, it is entirely compatible with the absence of any positive support for the victor. Take the example of the voter who in a final election votes for the victorious candidate of the opposite party because in a primary election the candidate of his party had won an interparty power struggle by means which the voter believed to be unfair. A vote for the victor in these circumstances is certainly not an expression of support. It is, rather, an effort to punish the losing candidate. Moreover, the voter might immediately begin to oppose the programs of the man for whom he voted, without any feelings of guilt.

It may be objected that the sustaining process may not be analogous to elections where there are opposing candidates, but it does resemble elections where there is a single slate of candidates. If it is not like a democratic election, it is like elections in single party states or more precisely elections in clubs and professional organizations where a nominating committee selects the nominees and the formal vote is mere ritual. The similarity of these procedures to the sustaining process is only superficial. In the case of most single party states, participation in the election is rarely voluntary and therefore the vote is empty of any commitment. What commitment exists in the case of clubs and professional organizations is usually to self-interest and therefore limited by the relevance of the organization to that interest. Membership in a civic organization may be the means of furthering a political career, business interests, or social aspirations without violating the fundamental nature of the civic club. Consequently, many members of these organizations view them in instrumental terms and, therefore, have no hesitation about using the organization to achieve interests which are not necessarily compatible with organizational goals.

Whatever it is, the sustaining vote is not an election— the Church member is not asked to choose between candidates, but whether he will support the nominee and his efforts to achieve the goals of the Church. While it is true some Mormons may be active Church members in order to advance their private interest, the considerable demands on members' time and financial resources usually become unbearable unless there is a deeper commitment than to purely selfish interests. The result is that most active members identify strongly with Church goals and do so for reasons that can only be understood in religious terms. In these circumstances the sustaining process becomes something more profound than the approval given by club members to a slate of officers suggested by a nominating committee.

The act of sustaining Church officers has meaning on two specific levels. On the first level, the raising of the hand is acknowledgment of the primacy of the Church's goals over a purely private interpretation of what those goals ought to be. It is, therefore, an explicit recognition of the legitimacy of the Church as the guardian of the gospel. Simultaneously it recognizes the right of the Church to determine the operational program to achieve gospel goals. Recognition of the Church's role is binding upon all participants in the sustaining process, which includes all members of the Church administrative structure. It is recognition of a set of common goals to which participating members give public support.

On the second level, the sustaining process is a public avowal of support for an individual office holder. As a sustaining vote for an individual officer, it means that members will provide both material and psychological support for him. Not only is he to be given a fair chance to succeed, but his success becomes a matter of personal concern of Church members in general as well as his subordinates. No assistance which can possibly aid his success is withheld; no barriers which might hinder his efforts are erected. Church members identify with the officer because they see him as an active agent and a co-worker in the realization of goals which they prize highly.

In addition to this identification of Church members and officers, the sustaining process legitimizes the officers. Legitimacy is generally thought to involve the delegation of certain powers and rights from one who holds these rights

and powers to another person. In this generally accepted
sense, legitimacy depends on the way an office holder is
viewed by his superior. An equally important view of legitimacy is the way in which an office holder is viewed by his
subordinates. It is this relationship which is vitally affected
by the sustaining process, since approval involves recognition
by potential subordinates that the office holder may rightfully make decisions which definitively determine their own
role in the organization. Furthermore the sustaining vote
commits the participating member to the notion that realization of organizational goals depends on the wholehearted support of individual office holders at every organizational level.

II

The sustaining process therefore symbolizes the existence
of an administrative environment in which both the leaders
and the subordinates simultaneously express loyalty to goals
of the Church and to each other. They both expect to achieve
their own personal needs as well as the goals of the Church
through a cooperative effort. On the part of the leaders
there is the knowledge, which comes if not by instinct then
by experience, that loyal subordinates are their most priceless
possession. Although too few leaders realize that they can
have loyal subordinates only if they are loyal to those they
supervise, in the Church environment loyalty for leaders
may persist long after it has ceased to be merited. This loyalty persists precisely because members are committed not only
to the specific leader, but to the gospel and Church as a
whole. The result is loyal behavior on the part of members,
even when the emotional, spiritual and psychological basis
for that loyalty no longer exists. In the long run, however,
there can be no double standard of loyalty; no leader can
long command respect and devotion if he does not begin with
respect and devotion for his subordinates. Christ's emphasis
on the need for mutual love as the basis for enduring human
relationships underlines this point sharply.

The unique administrative environment symbolized by the sustaining process creates for the Church leader unusual opportunities for creative leadership. To take advantage of these opportunities the leader must clearly understand that while in the secular world leaders must win the loyalty of subordinates, in the Church environment it already exists and therefore can only be lost. Loyalty to Church leadership exists primarily because individual Church members approach their callings with the pre-supposition that they will be loyal to those in authority. Their own orientation—reinforced by the sustaining process—is toward both organizational and personal loyalty. They are loyal, not because there is some external pressure on them, but because they have "internalized" a value system which includes loyalty to those in authority. They are loyal because being loyal satisfies their own image of how they ought to behave. In effect they say to themselves, "I believe I am loyal to Church leaders, but I need to translate that belief into action before my image of myself can be completely satisfactory."

Given this internalized sense of loyalty, members have a strong motive to look to leaders for guidance and direction, and do not ordinarily have to be coerced into accepting leadership. Furthermore, only the strongest possible provocation will drive them to oppose their own interpretations of Church goals and programs to those held by Church leaders. When this provocation becomes strong enough they will generally seek a release from their calling rather than enter into open confrontation, since this is the easiest way to reconcile the overwhelming need to be loyal with the equally strong desire to foster the success of Church programs.

Since the first administrative experience of most members of the Church is generally in some Church organization, they become sensitive at an early age to the expectation of loyalty which exists in that environment. These loyalty expectations are reinforced by attitudes transmitted to them by their parents, who themselves came under the influence of these expectations at an early age and whose experience in Church work has reinforced that influence. The result is, among committed members of the Church, a "Mormon" administrative style which is readily carried over into secular life. This style is characterized by a highly developed need to be loyal to employers and to the organizations for which they work. Therefore, if Mormons are good employees, as we are so often told by non-members—too often for our own good I sometimes think—it is not solely because they are hard workers or are well-trained, but because they bring to their task this strong sense of loyalty. Although this "Mormon" administrative style is relevant to the secular world, it has its greatest impact outside of the Church itself in Church related institutions such as Church schools. Faculty and employees of these institutions are particularly sensitive to the question of loyalty, since administrators of Church schools are assumed to be chosen in much the same way as are stake and ward leaders. Although there is no formal sustaining process for the leaders of these institutions, faculty and employees fully expect the same reciprocal loyalty to obtain in relationships as they have experienced in Church work. In a variety of ways, and in a variety of situations, then, the administrative style which members of the Church have learned in a Church context creates the anticipation that mutual loyalty will mark all administrative relationship. They have no greater sense of satisfaction than when that hope is fulfilled, nor no greater disappointment than its defeat.

III

In this context of institutional and personal loyalty, it is worthwhile to examine in some detail what kinds of behavior fall within the definition of loyal. What will a subordinate do or not do in his relations with those in authority, and what will leaders do or not do in their relations with subordinates? Although it is impossible to be exhaustive in listing acceptable behavior, perhaps some guide lines can be sketched out.

In what follows, I use the terms "leaders" and "subordinates" as convenient designations for the various offices in wards and stakes. Among the leadership positions, I envision stake and ward officers including superintendencies and presidencies of auxiliaries and priesthood officers. It is immediately obvious to those who understand the functioning of the Church that sometime all active members will be leaders.[1] What makes loyalty so vitally important, then, is not only its relationship to the successful fulfillment of the mission of the Church, but that only by the application of the "golden rule" as subordinates can members rightfully expect to command loyalty in leadership positions. Moreover, because there are so many tasks to be done in the Church, most members find themselves simultaneously subordinates as well as leaders. And it goes without saying that because of the hierarchal organization of the Church on a stake and ward basis, that all leaders from the President of the Church on down are both leaders and subordinates and therefore subject to the same requirements of loyalty.

First it might be noted that to show loyalty in subordinates is not a rubber stamp affair. It does mean that the subordinate *wants* the leader to succeed. To be successful the leader needs to feel useful, and respected as well as to feel that he has justified the confidence placed in him by those who have called him to his office; he needs to have a sense of accomplishment, to know that he has made a significant contribution to the success of the program of the Church. To be loyal, then, means that subordinates understand these elements of success and seek to support the leader in such a way as to assure that they will be attained. The loyal subordinate sees clearly the relevance to his own task of the paradox posed by Christ: that only those who lose their lives

---

[1]This paper deals with but one aspect of leadership. For a full discussion of leadership problems in a church context see Neal A. Maxwell, *A More Excellent Way* (Salt Lake City: Deseret Book Co., 1968).

shall find them. In his willing and selfless support of those
to whom he owes fealty, the subordinate will find his own
personal success experience. His goal, therefore, becomes, or
should become, to surrender when necessary his own desires
and views as to how the work should be pushed forward and
to give wholehearted support to those of the leader. He does
this without a "hidden agenda" because he understands that
unity of purpose and action is vital to the task of bringing
hearts unto God.

A second aspect of loyalty is a wholehearted participation in the work at hand. Broken down, this commitment
includes acceptance of difficult tasks without grumbling,
conscientious fulfillment of assignments, perseverance in the
face of disappointment, creative and innovative approaches
to problems, and a willingness to do what is necessary to get
the job done. Unless subordinates make these attributes the
touchstones of their behavior, loyalty threatens to remain
merely verbal. Everyone in positions of leadership in the
Church is familiar with the member who professes his support in private and well as in public, but who always has
some plausible excuse why the job is not done. Loyalty must
be marked by action, for action is after all the final measure
of fidelity. What ultimately mattered to Christ was not
Peter's affirmation of His divinity or his denial in the dark
hours before the crucifixion, but that when called to bear
witness Peter responded with his entire being, even though
it cost him his life. This is the ultimate commitment without which loyalty becomes merely a verbal ritual without
meaning.

I began this discussion of loyalty by saying that being
loyal was not the same as being a rubber stamp, for every
leader has need of counsel and advice. Because of this need
leaders in the Church are given counselors whose specific
task, along with sharing of the routine administrative burden, is to counsel with leaders. The loyal subordinate gives
this counsel openly and frankly. He speaks from his heart,

and out of his knowledge and experience. He is not afraid of saying, "I don't know." He does not merely tailor his views to what he thinks the leader wants to hear. He is, however, conscious of the burden of responsibility and therefore he weighs his advice carefully before giving it. But, above all, he is acutely aware of the thin, but distinct, line between counsel and harassment. Counsel looks forward and seeks opportunities where it can effectively influence programs and policies. Harassment looks backward to harp on mistakes and lost opportunities. Similarly, the loyal subordinate is quick to distinguish between constructive and negative criticism. He knows that the first is akin to counsel, for it seeks to learn from the past, and the second is a first cousin to harassment, for in its worst form it is only a crass means of self-aggrandizement. The loyal subordinate also knows that the distinction between these forms of criticism rests as much on those to whom it is directed as it does on the content of the criticism. Even the most helpful suggestions for improvement can be nothing less than carping criticism if they are constantly made, not to the leader, but to his subordinates or even to those who have no responsibility for the program. Criticism can only be constructive when it is timely made to those who have power to change what is being done, or who bear responsibility for the outcome. I think special emphasis should be placed on the *timely* aspect of constructive criticism, for where timeliness is absent, even constructive criticism runs the risk of being a rather subtle form of saying, "I told you so."

IV

If every leader had subordinates with the traits which characterize loyalty, few tasks in the Church would be insurmountable. The natural question, then, is under what conditions is a leader most likely to have such subordinates? In some cases, and perhaps more frequently, I believe, in the Church, than elsewhere, subordinates tend to be loyal regardless of the behavior of the leader. In the Church environment, such subordinates are generally those whose devotion to the gospel is sufficiently strong to transcend any personal resentment they may harbor toward the leader. The number of these subordinates is, however, relatively small; leaders would be unwise to expect continued support from subordinates regardless of the way they were treated. Each Church leader must approach his assignment with a clear understanding that most members of the Church are strongly predisposed toward personal and institutional loyalty; the leadership problem, therefore, is how to keep and to enhance that loyalty. Although it is true some members of the Church may prove disloyal subordinates regardless of the behavior of the leader, I believe on balance that the primary responsibility for fostering and building loyalty is a task of leadership. If this is true, Church leaders have a special responsibility to respond to their subordinates with a deep and abiding loyalty from which grows the bond of brotherhood so vital to the mission of the Church.

The first law of loyalty is, then, reciprocity. Leaders who are loyal to subordinates receive loyalty in return. The first step toward this reciprocal relationship requires the leader to believe, until proven otherwise in fairly explicit ways, that his subordinates are just as committed to Church goals as he is. Therefore, behavior of subordinates which appears on the surface to run counter to Church goals should be considered simply a failure to relate means to ends and not a rejection of those ends. A proposal by a young Sunday School teacher to have his class meet in the mountains on a Sunday morning can be seen by the superintendent in two different ways: (1) as a crass violation of the Sabbath or, (2) as a mistake in the selection of means to provide a spiritual experience for class members. I am suggesting that only by interpreting the teacher's behavior as a sincere, though perhaps somewhat mistaken effort to give his students a new spiritual experience can the superintendent maintain the loyalty and support symbolized in the sustaining process. If he interprets the teacher's action as a willful violation of the Sabbath, he challenges the depth of the teacher's commitment to the Church and begins thereby to undermine the sense of loyalty with which the teacher may actually have begun his task. On the other hand, if he undertakes to help the teacher realize that although his goal is worthwhile, the means selected to achieve that goal were not entirely appropriate, the bonds of loyalty are not impaired.

Perhaps no other behavior reveals so frankly the ultimate loyalty of the leader toward his subordinates as does his response to criticism of them by other subordinates or by outsiders. While his response can be complex and varied, it usually ranges between two extremes. At one end of the spectrum is the assumption by the leader that every negative criticism has a possible basis in truth. Since the charges explicit in the criticism may be true, then the criticism ought to be investigated to determine its validity. Those who espouse this view argue that if the criticism proves false, the leader is reassured and the subordinate vindicated; if it is valid then corrective action may still be taken while minimum action is required. The attitude at the other end of the spectrum is to reject all criticism of subordinates in much the same manner that fathers and mothers are apt to reject out of hand the possibility that their children are guilty of grave faults.

Both of these extremes are replete with dangers which should dissuade the perceptive leader from embracing either of them. The first can only create an atmosphere of suspicion and mistrust. How often does a subordinate have to prove himself? Are there no distinctions to be made as to kinds and sources of criticism? For subordinates to be effective they must be sure that they will not be subjected to harrassment by captious critics. If every allegation is to be investigated, if every critic who does not agree with what is done or said is to be given serious audience, no subordinate can ever feel that he enjoys the leaders' confidence and trust, and yet no factor is more important to his ultimate success. In the face of repeated investigation of every alleged wrong, subordinates will gradually reduce the vision of their calling until they are doing only what is necessary and that only in ways carefully supervised by the leader. In the end when the last hope of fostering a relationship of trust and confidence with the leader is gone, they either ask for a release or persist in hopes that a change in leadership will restore the conditions necessary to the optimal performance of their task.

The dangers of the second extreme—rejection of all criticism of subordinates—are no less real. The responsibilities of leadership include not only the need to assure loyal subordinates, but also the necessity to build effective Church programs. The leader therefore shares a responsibility to those who called him to his office and to those members who are dependent on him for the success of Church programs. The superintendent of a Sunday School must simultaneously achieve three goals. He must satisfy the bishopric; he must meet the demands of the students for teachers who bring spiritual direction into their lives; and he must support and defend the teachers so as to assure their loyalty for him and for the Sunday School. It is rare that all of these goals can be achieved simultaneously, and where it is impossible, some decisions must be made as to what should be given preference. There are no hard fast rules to guide the leader in these situations; he must gather as much information as he can, consult past experiences, and ultimately rely on prayer. If he were to reject all criticism of the teachers in the Sunday School as being unworthy of his notice, then he runs the risk that he will be unfaithful to his other responsibilities. Every Church leader, therefore, if he is to integrate loyalty into his administrative style in meaningful ways must be alert to the problems presented by the criticism of his subordinates.

Perhaps the first step toward a successful response to the problems presented by criticism is to be fully aware that very few people can fulfill a Church position without generating some criticism. Therefore, the existence of some criticism should not be taken as evidence that the subordinate under fire has serious faults. The leader who is easily embarrassed and who panics at the slightest criticism of subordinates will always find it difficult to create a relationship of trust with subordinates. If leaders understand that some critics are never satisfied, they are more likely to retain the serenity of spirit required to deal calmly and temperately with this delicate problem of human relations.

A second attitude which helps to put criticism in its proper perspective is that the burden of proof is on the critic. "Every man is innocent until proven guilty" is a time honored maxim which is frequently violated, but which must be given full credit by leaders who wish to have loyal subordinates. The first response of every leader, it seems to me, should be to examine the possible motives hidden behind the criticism and, therefore, to reserve judgment as to the credibility of the criticism until it is clear that the critic comes with a clean hand and a pure heart.

There are many types of criticism, some of which are easily recognized. Some is a natural result of the proprietary attitude which many members have toward the Church. This is the kind of "in-house" grousing that one finds in families and other small groups. For the most part it is harmless and not intended to do evil; it can usually be stilled by a gentle reminder that we all have faults. Some criticism comes from habitual critics who satisfy their own insecurity by faultfinding, and some from those who have inadequate knowledge. Finally, some criticism comes from those who are deeply interested in prompting the effectiveness of Church programs.

It is one of the minor paradoxes of Church work that criticism from sincerely concerned and obviously loving critics is the only meritorious criticism and the rarest. It is rarest because frequent reaction of the committed member of the

Church to what they consider an inadequate performance is
to give increased support to ward or stake officers or teachers in hopes that this additional support will help solve the
problem. Moreover, they are frequently right in doing so.
Consequently sincere criticism is limited by the selflessness
of those who might legitimately make it. Because it is the
only meritorious criticism it must be listened to with care
while that of the carping member must be scorned. But it is
not always easy to distinguish between the two, and therefore, patience and discernment are the qualities most needed
by Church leaders. Much harm has been done by leaders
who have accepted too readily the correctness of criticism
of subordinates. Much good has come where administrators
have turned criticism aside with an expression of full support
for subordinates. Expressions of trust and confidence in face
of criticism will certainly deter those critics who are testing
the limits of the leader's support of subordinates. It will
rarely discourage the sincere critic who has given his full
support and sympathy, but who is driven by his deep concern for the success of the program to express openly his
criticism of an officer or teacher.

V

Thoughtful reflection on the impact of loyalty on lead-
er-subordinate relationships in the Church context leads one
back ultimately to the Prophet Joseph Smith. Perhaps no
words of his are more often quoted than his response to the
question as to how he governed his people: "I teach them
correct principles and they govern themselves." There is no
statement on leadership that has more profound implications
than this short sentence. What it says in effect is that the
Prophet considered his people to be intelligent, rational, responsible human beings. Their intelligence was manifested
in their ability to grasp and understand correct principles.
They could discern between good and evil, right and wrong;
they could rise above their provincial surroundings and their

limited education to appreciate the spiritual vistas opened to them by an understanding of correct principles. Their rationality was reflected in their ability to relate means to ends and to choose from among all the competing ways of doing things those means calculated to most effectively realize the right principles they had been taught. Moreover, they could do this by themselves because they were endowed with initiative, with perseverance and with love of each other, without which community life is a burden, not a joy. Their responsibility was evinced by the gift of freedom to govern themselves. Because they were responsible, they could be trusted to use their freedom to build the kingdom of God out of love and not out of fear. Because they were responsible, they could be granted freedom with the assurance that they would strive not only for knowledge but also for wisdom.

It is in this spirit that all Church leaders should approach their subordinates. If leaders consider their subordinates indolent, lacking in responsibility, self-centered, without initiative, disloyal, resistant to change, in all probability that is the kind of subordinates they will have. The moral of the "eight cow wife" is not a fairy tale for children, but a living reality. The chickens do come home to roost. A leader may achieve some success by driving subordinates, by using the method of "divide and rule," but if he does, his passing from the scene will be greeted by his subordinates with sighs of relief and he will slip unloved into memory.

Only those leaders who see their subordinates as possessing not only a testimony of the gospel, but also the capacity to assume responsibility, the intelligence to appreciate the goals of the Church, the wisdom to understand that both leaders and subordinates can find satisfaction and ultimately salvation only through an integration of their lives in service to others, will have fully loyal subordinates. Leaders who doubt the loyalty of their subordinates generally have to look no further than their own hearts for the cause of their doubts. Christ pierced to the heart of the matter: he who would be "chief among you, let him be your servant. . . ." Unless this truth is taken to heart and transferred into action, no leader will be able to benefit fully from the treasury of loyalty which is bequeathed to him by his calling. To respond to that loyalty is to testify to our love and truth for our fellowmen, to squander that treasure through ambition, self-seeking and a lust for power is the ultimate betrayal of the gospel. "We have learned by sad experience," Joseph Smith observed, "that it is the nature and disposition of almost all men as soon as they get a little authority as they suppose, they will immediately begin to exercise unrighteous dominion." No other warning should be necessary to those who are called to positions of authority in the Church. What is common among men should be uncommon in the Church, and yet the prophet's experience was with leaders in the Church. The full implication is, therefore, readily apparent. Leadership in the Church is a difficult task and chances for failure are many, but the rewards are great to those who have the courage to base their leadership on respect and love for the gospel, for the Church, and for those whose work they oversee. Some of these rewards can be inherited only in the future, but one is immediately redeemable: loyal subordinates whose love, respect and support make leadership an experience of ineffable joy through which we glimpse, beyond the clouds of mortality, a vision of that divine devotion and love that led Christ to Calvary.

Oliver Cowdery, Esq.: His Non-Church Decade

Richard Lloyd Anderson

RICHARD L. ANDERSON, professor of history and religion at Brigham Young University, has written widely on Church history subjects. He holds three graduate degrees: an M.A. from BYU, a D. Jp. from Harvard, and Ph.D. from California University at Berkeley. This selection, "Oliver Cowdery, Esq." shows the integrity and contribution of Oliver Cowdery during the approximately ten years he was out of the Church.

Dr. Anderson has written numerous articles and papers, and most recently published a book, *Joseph Smith's New England Heritage* (Deseret Book Co., 1972).

His wife is the former Carma de Jong and they have four children.

OLIVER COWDERY, ESQ.:
HIS NON-CHURCH DECADE

Richard Lloyd Anderson

Oliver Cowdery can be considered the co-founder of Mormonism, for no one else was so intimately associated with Joseph Smith in the formative years of the LDS movement. Before his death in 1850, he called himself the "oldest member of the Church," meaning that no one else then knew the realities of The Church of Jesus Christ of Latter-day Saints as well as he. The study of the phenomenon of Mormonism through the biography of Joseph Smith is incomplete, for the reason that Cowdery claimed to share every early spiritual experience with the Prophet. Cowdery was alienated but later returned to the migrating Saints at Kanesville, where he reiterated earlier statements concerning the supernatural basis of the Mormon religion.

Until the publication of Stanley Gunn's *Oliver Cowdery*, there was little factual data available concerning the decade between Oliver Cowdery's excommunication in 1838 and his return in 1848. That biography established locations and activities of this period in his life. The further research reported here has extended such data, but of more importance it has recovered evaluations of Cowdery's career from several men in public life who knew him. "Oliver Cowdery, Esquire," is the single title that sums up his vocation, for he was respected by fellow attorneys as an astute legal craftsman. But he was also a politician, journalist, promoter of education, and public servant. The picture of a man of considerable stature emerges from the review of what he did professionally, apart from the Mormon people and what his associates in that period thought of him personally.

Cowdery's excommunication from the Mormon Church in April of 1838 was the culmination of dissent for some time from what he termed in an official letter "the outward government of this church."[1] When friction over Church policies came to a head, he looked for a place of settlement in Missouri "where a county seat will eventually be located."[2] Although ideas for a possible newspaper edited by Cowdery had developed quite far, definite plans for law practise had been made. In a letter of January 1838, he inventoried a basic frontier law library, and disclosed that an additional fifty-five volumes of law books had been ordered.[3] In March, Cowdery wrote to his brothers, then also embarking on law careers, "I am pursuing my study as fast as health and circumstances will permit."[4] By June of that year, his correspondence expresses disappointment in lack of delivery of his additional law volumes, but reveals that he cannot visit Kirtland because (in part), "I . . . feel the importance of improving every moment with books."[5] With his strong feelings of family unity, he made an appeal for a common area of settlement with his brothers, and stated his ideal of competence as a lawyer:

> I take no satisfaction in thinking of practicing law with a half dozen books. Let us get where people live, with a splendid library, attend strictly to our books and practice, and I have no fear if life and health are spared, but we can do as well as, at least, the middle class.[6]

---

[1]Letter of Oliver Cowdery to Edward Partridge, April 12, 1838, Far West, Mo., copied into Far West Record (LDS Historian's Office), typescript p. 115, also cited in Joseph Smith, *History of The Church of Jesus Christ of Latter-day Saints*, ed. B. H. Roberts (Salt Lake City, Utah, 1946-1950), 3:18.

[2]Letter of Oliver Cowdery to Brothers Warren and Lyman, Feb. 4, 1838, Far West, Mo. This is part of a letter collection from the Oliver Cowdery Letter Book, in possession of the Huntington Library. All quotations in the article are exact from the documents cited, with editorial corrections limited to spelling, capitalization, and punctuation.

[3]Letter of Oliver Cowdery to Warren Cowdery, Jan. 21, 1838, Far West, Mo. (Huntington Library).

[4]Letter of Oliver Cowdery to Brothers Warren and Lyman, Mar. 1838, Far West, Mo. (Huntington Library).

[5]Ibid.

[6]Letter of Oliver Cowdery to Brothers Warren and Lyman, June 2, 1838, Far West, Mo., photographic copy in Stanley R. Gunn, *Oliver Cowdery* (Salt Lake City, Utah: Bookcraft, 1962), p. 266.

Giving up the idea of practising in Missouri, and then experimenting with a move to Springfield, Illinois, Oliver Cowdery united with his family at Kirtland, Ohio, where his brothers Warren and Lyman lived. He was still in Missouri in late August, when a letter from Lyman impatiently pleads with him to come to Kirtland.[7] Thomas Marsh remembered talking with Cowdery in the late autumn, at least October.[8] But by November 21, 1838, Cowdery had arrived in Kirtland, where his name appears as secretary of an organizing meeting of the "Western Reserve Teachers Seminary and Kirtland Institute."[9]

The year 1839 was very clearly spent in Kirtland, Ohio. There are over a score of references to Oliver Cowdery in the year 1839, all of which show him to have lived in Kirtland. For instance, he appears in 1839-1840 in the Kirtland Township minutes, once as clerk of the meeting.[10] He was prominent politically in the Democratic Party. The Geauga County Convention that year chose Cowdery as one of thirteen delegates to the bi-county senatorial convention.[11] An upset victory for Benjamin Bissell, prominent Painesville attorney, took place. This is of interest because Bissell was earlier retained by the Mormons and is probably the source for the recommendation of Oliver Cowdery to the Democrats of Tiffin, Ohio, the site of his main non-Mormon career.

Cowdery's law practise began in earnest in Kirtland. Judge William Lang, who knew him intimately in Tiffin, said that Cowdery studied under Bissell and then was admit-

---

[7]Letter of Lyman Cowdery to Oliver Cowdery, August 21, 1838, Kirtland, Ohio. (Beineke Library, Yale University).

[8]Thomas B. Marsh, "History of Thomas Baldwin Marsh," written Nov. 1857 (LDS Historian's Office); a convenient reprint is found in *Millennial Star*, Vol. 26 (1864), p. 406. Marsh's narrative indicates that he left Far West in August, 1838 but did not see Cowdery until some time later in Richmond. But Marsh had probably not been in Richmond long when made his affidavit there on Oct. 24, 1838, and LDS records place both Marsh and Hyde (who attested his affidavit) in Far West until October. Also, the affidavit of Marsh describes events of October and indicates their immediately recent nature.

[9]*Painesville* (Ohio) *Telegraph*, Nov. 29, 1838.

[10]Original minutes at the Lake County Historical Society, Mentor, Ohio; microfilm at Brigham Young University.

[11]*Painesville Republican*, Sept. 26 and October 3, 1839.

ted to the Ohio Bar on examination. As stated, Cowdery's residence was Kirtland in the year 1839. Since no law activities appear before early 1840, one might speculate on what he did for a living that year. His sketch in the Cowdery family history was based in part on contact with his widow, Elizabeth Whitmer Cowdery, who lived until 1892. It says that he "supported himself by teaching school while pursuing his study of the law."[12] If this sentence is strictly accurate, he taught school in Kirtland during the year 1839. Legal activity is in evidence from the beginning of the year 1840. Oliver Cowdery does not appear as a dues-paying attorney in 1839, but he is assessed as a "practising lawyer" in 1840 by the County Commissioners.[13] The first case of "L & O. Cowdery" was advertised in the *Painesville Republican* January 20, 1840, and a scanning of the legal sources reveals other cases in the first half of that year by these full brothers who practised as "brothers-in-law."[14]

The transfer of Oliver Cowdery's law practise from Kirtland to Tiffin, Ohio, during the year 1840 must be attributed in large part to his editorial experience. It is interesting that his Missouri letters two years before this indicate more confidence in journalism than law: "were it editing a paper, or writing an article for the public eye, I should feel perfectly at home."[15] Such a comment is based upon almost six years of fairly continuous service as an editor of Church newspapers. He was associated with W. W. Phelps in the publication of the first LDS newspaper, *The Evening and the Morning Star*, in Missouri and was sole editor of it in

---

[12]Mary Bryant Alverson Mehling, *Cowderey — Cowdery — Cowdray Genealogy*, (New York, [1911]), p. 173. This book was printed privately in the New York City area in the early years of this century, but p. 173 indicates contact was made in 1887 with Elizabeth Whitmer Cowdery, who furnished the genealogy dates for the family and probably some biographical data.

[13]Lake County Commissioners Record, Book A, entry of June 1, 1840.

[14]See *Painesville Republican*, Jan. 28, 1840; Court of Common Pleas Record, Geauga Co., Ohio, Book X, pp. 449-52 (microfilm at LDS Genealogical Society, Salt Lake City); Court of Common Pleas Record, Lake Co., Ohio, Book A, pp. 109-10; *Painesville Republican*, June 4, 1840.

[15]Letter of Oliver Cowdery to Brothers Warren and Lyman, June 2, 1838, photographic reproduction in Gunn, *op. cit.*, 264.

Kirtland, editor of the successor-newspaper, *Latter Day Saints' Messenger and Advocate,* and the secular (and Democratic) *Northern Times,* both of which were published in Kirtland at the height of the Mormon concentration there.

Some 125 miles to the southeast, on the Sandusky river, was Tiffin, Ohio, the center of Seneca County. In 1840, the township in which Tiffin stood had a population of some 2,000,[16] and the county some 18,000.[17] The "rip-roaring" campaign of 1840 was underway when a group of dedicated and vigorous democrats imported a press and sought an editor. Probably on the recommendation of Benjamin Bissell, Cowdery was promised this job. A prominent Tiffin politician, who was certainly in a position to know, later reminisced, "Oliver Cowdery was to have been editor, but was dropped on the discovery that he was one of the seven founders of Mormonism."[18] If the legendary seven sages are confused with the mathematics of Mormon origins, the point is that Cowdery was brought to Tiffin to hold the critical post of editor of a party paper, an action that would not have been accomplished without recommendation of party leaders elsewhere and a personal interview.[19] Cowdery as a person was evidently impressive enough to be given responsibility, but a Book of Mormon witness was obviously unacceptable politically.

The above incident took place in the summer of 1840. Reminiscences and the 1840 census prove that Cowdery ig-

---

[16]Consul W. Butterfield, *History of Seneca County* (Sandusky, Ohio, 1848), p. 82.

[17]William Lang, *History of Seneca County* (Springfield, Ohio, 1880), p. 633.

[18]"Letter from General W. H. Gibson," *Seneca Advertiser* (Tiffin, Ohio), April 12, 1892.

[19]The tradition in Tiffin concerning Cowdery's prior law connections identified him as studying under Benjamin Bissell of Painesville. (Lang. *op. cit.*, p. 364.) Whether this is strictly true (Cowdery lived during this period in Kirtland, not Painesville), it undoubtedly preserves the memory of the connection between the two men. Cowdery knew Bissell well in Kirtland as Joseph Smith's personal attorney and as a delegate to the bi-county convention in 1839 voted for Bissell's nomination as state senator. Since Cowdery was previously unknown at Tiffin, contact was undoubtedly first made with Cowdery through party leaders in the Cleveland region.

nored the rebuff of being dismissed as a Mormon and nevertheless opened a law practise that was to last seven years in
Tiffin. The court records and the papers signed by Cowdery
still on file in Tiffin show that his legal practise was substantial.[20] Stanley Gunn has listed only representative cases for
this period. But Cowdery as an individual is not found in
the archaic rhetoric of legal pleadings. He does emerge clearly
in the recollections of two fellow attorneys, a profession
whose members are quite as critical of each other as are historians.

The colleague who wrote most about him is probably
the one man in Tiffin who knew him better than anyone
else. This is William Lang, lawyer, politician, and author.
He held local offices of prosecuting attorney and probate
judge. He was first mayor of Tiffin and County Treasurer
for two terms. He served two terms in the Ohio Senate. He
was democratic candidate for lieutenant governor, and in
1880, candidate for secretary of state, receiving 47% of the
vote as Ohio went Republican that year. As an author, Lang
produced in his *History of Seneca County* one of the unusual
county histories that is more than eulogy. He writes with the
warmth of a neighbor but the critical eye of a seasoned attorney. He should have known Cowdery well, since he ap-
prenticed in Cowdery's office for a year and a half.[21] As a
matter of fact, he risked his life by going into the burning
courthouse for valuable files at Cowdery's request.[22] Lang
entered the Ohio bar in 1842, and after that had five years'
association with Cowdery as a fellow attorney. The fore-
going contact, which Lang characterized as intimate, brought
him nothing but admiration for the "noble and true man-
hood" of Cowdery. The main details of his professional evaluation are as follows:

----

[20]Although Gunn found no documentation of Cowdery's law cases prior to
1842, the *Van Burenite and Seneca County Advertiser* of March 12, 1841 carries
a publication notice of an action in which Cowdery was counsel.
[21]Lang, *op. cit.*, p. 387.
[22]Ibid., 179.

Mr. Cowdery was an able lawyer and a great advocate. His manners were easy and gentlemanly; he was polite, dignified, yet courteous. . . . His association with others was marked by the great amount of information his conversation conveyed and the beauty of his musical voice. His addresses to the court and jury were characterized by a high order of oratory, with brilliant and forensic force.[23]

The second attorney who put in writing his recollections of Cowdery was William Harvey Gibson. Perhaps it is enough of an introduction to observe that his statue stands before the courthouse in Tiffin. He is not represented as a general, though he held this status as a campaigner of merit in the Civil War. But he stands in the role of an orator, for he was nationally recognized in Republican circles as a campaign speaker in the late nineteenth century. Gibson was a young lawyer like Lang at the time that Cowdery practised in Tiffin. Though Gibson was involved in a state scandal and resigned as treasurer of Ohio in 1857, by all reports he redeemed himself and won back a credible reputation in the balance of the nineteenth century. Since he was an active attorney from 1845 to 1872, his opinion of Cowdery as a lawyer is of value. The guarantee of objectivity is found in the fact that Gibson as an early Whig was a political opponent of the man he speaks about. In a letter for publication in 1892, Gibson said, "Cowdery was an able lawyer and [an] agreeable, irreproachable gentleman."[24] Several anti-Mormon sources have published portions of private correspondence from Gibson on Cowdery's life in Tiffin. One letter to Thomas Gregg is evidently authentic, because it fits Gibson's style and because Gregg is known to have sent inquiries to those who knew the early figures and events of Mormonism. In this letter, Gibson gives a very similar statement to the one that he personally published about Cowdery:

---

[23]Ibid., 365.
[24]"Letter from General W. H. Gibson," *Seneca Advertiser* (Tiffin, Ohio), April 12, 1892.

"He was an able lawyer, a fine orator, a ready debater and led a blameless life, while residing in this city."[25]

Cowdery's published biography has sketched his community activities in Tiffin. Not mentioned is his election in 1843 as chairman of the first Hook and Ladder Company, an organization established two years after the courthouse caught fire and was largely destroyed in the absence of such a fire department. Cowdery and his law partner, Joel Wilson, had suffered the loss of their papers then, since their office was in the courthouse. Appointment to many other civic committees shows Oliver Cowdery's prominence. But his most solid contribution was regular service as a member of the Board of School Examiners of Seneca County.[26] Not only are notices and proceedings of the board published, signed by Oliver Cowdery, but two individuals leave recollections of being examined by Cowdery for teaching certificates, William Lang, and the future wife of William H. Gibson, Martha Creeger. A literate spokesman for professionalism watched Cowdery and the others who examined Miss Creeger and reported in a published letter, "I must acknowledge myself not a little instructed, although but a spectator."[27] Cowdery was a natural educator. Case files in the Tiffin courthouse disclose that he also served as chairman of three-man committees for examining candidates for admission to the bar.

Since politics is the most public of all activities, Cowdery's prominence in this arena presents the historical equivalent of a searchlight on the man in his non-Mormon decade. What is revealed is not only energetic public service, but a great deal of personal tenacity in the face of scorn. A basic list of his political appointments at Tiffin can be compiled

---

[25]Letter of William H. Gibson to Thomas Gregg, August 3, 1882, Tiffin, Ohio, *cit.* Charles A. Shook, *The True Origin of the Book of Mormon* (Cincinnati, 1914), p. 57. On the following page, Shook indicates that he has copied this (and other Tiffin letters) "directly from the originals."

[26]See Lang, *op. cit.*, p. 330, and Martha Creeger Gibson, *Reminiscences of the Early Days of Tiffin, Ohio.*

[27]*Seneca Advertiser*, Oct. 14, 1842.

from files of contemporary newspapers. In making such a summary, it would be inconvenient to itemize every speech on public or partisan occasions. Merely reading an inventory of offices would not accurately convey the frequency of his community participation or his general reputation as an articulate party spokesman, symbolized by ratification meeting at Tiffin on behalf of Democratic national candidates in 1844, at which "O. Cowdery, Esq., was loudly called for" and responded with "a few brief but eloquent remarks."[28] Nevertheless, the bare summary of his appointments at Tiffin displays a record of reliable political service:[29]

1842

Delegate to County Convention (chairman of address and resolutions committee)

Delegate to District Convention (chairman of address and resolutions committee)

1844

Delegate to County Convention (reported resolutions)

Appointed to County Central Committee for Year

Delegate to District Convention

Member of "Informing Committee" (prominent speakers group)

1845

Elected One of Three Township Trustees (with Democrats winning by about 250 to 200 votes)

Delegate to County Convention (reported resolutions)

Delegate to State Convention

1846

Chairman of Resolutions Committee, County Rally

Appointed to County Central Committee for Year

Candidate for State Senator at Tri-County Convention (received 15% of delegates' votes on two ballots)

---

[28]Ibid., June 14, 1844.

[29]The offices listed are found in the *Seneca Advertiser* on the following dates: Aug. 26, Sept. 2, 1842; Aug. 23, Aug. 30, 1844; April 11, Aug. 1, Sept. 5, Dec. 26, 1845; Feb. 6, July 10, Aug. 7, 1846.

Cowdery's political career was characterized by setbacks. In a private letter, William Lang, fellow attorney and fellow Democrat, summed up his public vulnerability as follows:

> Cowdery was a Democrat and a most powerful advocate of the principles of the party on the stump. For this he became the target of the Whig stumpers and press, who denounced him as a Mormon and made free use of C.'s certificate at the end of the Mormon Bible to crush his influence. He suffered great abuse for this while he lived here on that account.[30]

Although the Whig papers of this Tiffin era are incompletely preserved, there are some clear illustrations of such attacks. For instance, to put over the point that a prominent Whig had uttered nonsense in a speech, the *Seneca Advertiser* reported it "verbatim" with several lines of randomly disordered type. The Whig answer was a jibe at Cowdery: "As it is in an 'unknown tongue,' the *reporter* could have been none other than one of Joe Smith's disciples. We beseech the editor to persuade him to come out and give us the interpretation of it in English . . ."[31] Yet it is clear that the Book of Mormon witness was an asset rather than a liability to the Democrats of Seneca County.

Oliver Cowdery's staunchest defender was John Breslin, who as a young man fell heir to the editorial post that Cowdery was initially offered. Breslin was an accomplished infighter in local politics, with a special ability to reach the German vote of his county. Breslin was then one of the brilliant young men of Ohio politics, serving two terms in the Ohio house of representatives, where he was elected speaker. The culmination and termination of his political career came after his election as state treasurer in 1856. Following practises of some predecessors, he privately invested substantial state funds that turned out to be uncollectable.

---

[30]Letter of William Lang to Thomas Gregg, Nov. 5, 1881, Tiffin, Ohio, *cit.* Shook, *op. cit.*, p. 56; cf. n. 25.
[31]*Tiffin Gazette*, Oct. 6, 1842.

Since it is doubtful that he profited personally, his defense of poor judgment is probably correct. The shipwreck of his career affected likewise his successor in office, William Gibson, who, as his fellow-townsman and brother-in-law, bought time for Breslin at the risk of his own reputation by not reporting the deficit on taking office. Breslin's later mistake is quite irrelevant to his opinion of Cowdery. As editor, he reported Cowdery's activities, promoted his reputation as a capable public speaker, and openly defended him when attacked by the Whig press. He even found Cowdery's past experience in publishing of value. This was something of a vindication of the man who was too tainted with Mormonism to be editor in 1840. In 1846 and 1847 he was entrusted for several months with that job because Breslin was in attendance at the Ohio legislature and requested Cowdery to be temporary editor of the *Seneca Advertiser*. After returning from the state capital, Beslin published the following appreciation:

> In looking over the columns of the Advertiser, published during our absence, we felt impelled to congratulate our readers upon the interest and ability parted them by our friend, Mr. COWDERY, to whom we entrusted the management of our paper. Mr. C. has conducted it in a manner wholly satisfactory to ourselves, and we doubt not to our readers, and our thanks are due him for his attention and kindness.[32]

At this point in life, Cowdery planned a change of residence to Elkhorn, Wisconsin, where his brother Lyman had moved from Kirtland. The letters of Oliver in Tiffin contain allusions to sickness from a damp climate (perhaps chronic tuberculosis), no doubt the foremost reason for the move. By summer of 1847, Breslin printed a series of letters from Cowdery in Wisconsin, reporting on the political excitement of the transition from territorial to state government.

The successful lawyer did not enter Wisconsin Territory as a refugee, but as a man of established reputation car-

---

[32]*Seneca Advertiser*, Feb. 19, 1847.

rying credentials. He made immediate contacts with community leaders.[33] On the basis of party service, he at once
entered the friendship of Horace A. Tenney, publisher of
the *Wisconsin Argus*. The letter is still preserved that John
Breslin wrote to "Dear Tenney" recommending "my friend,
O. Cowdery, Esq. of this place":

> Since my residence here we have been on terms of intimate personal
> and political friendship. He is a gentleman of honor, integrity and talents,
> and should he conclude to locate in your state, you will find him an accept-
> able auxiliary to the Democratic Party, and, no doubt, to yourself a valued
> friend.[34]

After his first contacts in the territorial capital, Cowdery wrote Tenney that he might yet move to Madison, but
was seriously considering Elkhorn on the urging of "many
of my former acquaintances" there. He stated that his decision was to be based on "business, health, etc." More personal
considerations of friendship evidently dictated the move to
Elkhorn, where there was the close relationship with his
brother Lyman and family, hinted at in this Tenney letter.
By the autumn of 1847 Oliver Cowdery had moved his family to Elkhorn. Some human interest glimmers from the
minutes of the Walworth County Commission, October 8,
1847:

> On motion resolved: That Oliver Cowdery have the privilege of
> occupying the northwest corner room of the courthouse at the rate of
> fifteen dollars to be paid into the county treasury quarterly, provided that
> such occupancy does not interfere with the present officer occupying the
> same or the jury.[35]

Cowdery's profession in Wisconsin was of course still law.
The legal archaeologist may discover Cowdery cases in the

---

[34]Letter of John W. Breslin to H. A. Tenney, April 6, 1847, Tiffin, Ohio
(State Historical Society of Wisconsin).
[35]Walworth County Commissioners' Minutes, Book 2, Oct. 8, 1847.
[33]On May 18, 1847, Cowdery wrote from Wisconsin indicating that he was
making contacts in Madison and reported a congenial conversation with David
Irvin, a judge of the territorial supreme court. *Seneca Advertiser*, June 18, 1847.

court journals at Elkhorn, and the two known issues of the *Walworth County Democrat* of this period carry the notice of "O. Cowdery, Attorney & Counsellor at Law."

If Cowdery moved to Wisconsin to improve his health, he was not without motivation to improve his political status. Positions of prominence were more accessible in the less structured relationships of the territory then graduating to statehood. In the spring of 1848 a letter discloses that his brother Lyman had promoted legislation to authorize Oliver to make an index of the territorial statutes. Such a bill passed the Council but not the House, showing that the Cowdery brothers carried some influence in Wisconsin political circles. Further proof of this consists of extant letters of both men to Charles M. Baker, a key figure in regional patronage in southern Wisconsin.[36]

Early 1848 was the time of election of the first officials in Wisconsin under its state constitution, and Oliver Cowdery emerged as a local leader of his party with less than a year of residence in the new location. In April 1848, he was nominated as Democratic candidate for Assemblyman from the Elkhorn region of Walworth County. Although the full details of the campaign have perished with the disappearance of the two party papers in Elkhorn during the campaign, a systematic search of other Wisconsin papers makes it possible to reconstruct main public comment upon Cowdery. The Whig paper at Elkhorn, the *Western Star*, acknowledged his candidacy by noting that he was one of the three witnesses of the Book of Mormon. A surviving article dependant upon this Elkhorn story undoubtedly follows the style and vocabulary of Cowdery's political opponents in associating him with the "Mormon Bible," "Joe Smith," and when it drops the obvious hint that Cowdery's "Whig competitor" is "an estimable citizen, well qualified for the office, and not a believer in Mormonism."[37] At the peak of the short

---

[36]These are on file at the State Historical Society of Wisconsin.
[37]*Milwaukee Sentinel*, April 13, 1848.

campaign, the Elkhorn *Star* copied, "for Cowdery's and the People's edification, sundry extracts from the Mormon Bible," among which was certainly his signed testimony. One's imagination is not taxed to envision the comments then printed. The Whig paper from the neighboring county, the *Milwaukee Sentinel,* chose a patronizing sarcasm:

> Our contemporary, we think, should deal more leniently with Mr. Cowdery's "youthful indiscretions." In testifying to the divine origin of Mormonism, he did not attempt half so great an imposition, as in now seeking to palm off "Loco-Focoism" as genuine democracy.[38]

Though Cowdery's party largely carried the county, he was not elected. In the face of the degree of prejudice against him, his small margin of defeat is impressive. By estimate, the votes cast in his district were about 500, and he lost by 40.[39] What is remarkable about the campaign is the public support given by his friends during and after the defeat, when either apologies or silence were alternatives. At Cowdery's first arrival in Wisconsin, he had talked and corresponded with Horace A. Tenney, a Madison resident whose later life was one of distinguished though not famous public service. Tenney then held part ownership of the *Wisconsin Argus,* a Democratic paper in Madison of statewide influence. The *Argus* not only defended Cowdery during the campaign, but expressed sharp regret at the religious grounds of his defeat: "He is a man of sterling integrity, sound and vigorous intellect, and every way worthy, honest and capable."[40] Repercussions of the campaign were most loudly heard in Tiffin, Ohio, where Breslin and correspondent "Q" responded with public indignation at the slander of their "esteemed friend and former fellow citizen, O. Cowdery, Esq." The following quote is part of Breslin's spirited defense, "O. Cowdery, Esq.", published first in the *Seneca Advertiser,*

---

[38]Ibid., April 29, 1848.
[39]See *Daily Wisconsin* (Milwaukee), May 11, 1848: "Kelsey (Whig), over Cowdery, 40 majority." Total vote estimate is based on examination of extant election returns.
[40]*Wisconsin Argus,* May 16, 1848.

then reprinted in the *Walworth County Democrat,* and finally picked up in a gesture of vindication after the campaign by Tenney's *Wisconsin Argus:*

> Mr. C. was a resident among us for a period of seven years, during which time he earned himself an enviable distinction at the bar of this place and of this judicial circuit, as a sound and able lawyer, and as a citizen none could have been more esteemed. His honesty, integrity, and industry were worthy the imitation of all, whilst his unquestioned legal abilities reflected credit as well upon himself as upon the profession of which he was a member.[41]

Prior to Cowdery's political bid in Wisconsin, he had laid firm plans to rejoin the migrating Mormons in the Council Bluffs area. Hoping to visit the Church at Winter Quarters for the anniversary conference of April 6, 1848, the former "second elder" wrote his warmest letter out of the Church to "Dear Brigham," at the same time indicating a delay by reason of "certain business" that "I may find myself under an honorable obligation of doing." This language must refer to the bill then under consideration to award Cowdery up to $650 for making a "complete index" to the territorial laws.[42] Subsequently the Assemblyman nomination took place, and it is obvious that a man of his ability would not want to pass the recognition (and in a sense vindication) of his considerable political labors of the past decade. Yet it is striking that in the midst of the campaign for that office Cowdery disclosed to his intimate friend (and brother-in-law) Phineas Young that it was only critical sickness that kept him from uniting with the Church on April 6 as planned, since "I dared not undertake the journey." This same letter is notable for the single unexplained

---

[41]*Seneca Advertiser,* May 5, 1848, recopied with additional favorable comments by *Wisconsin Argus,* May 30, 1848.

[42]Letter of Oliver Cowdery to Phineas Young, Mar. 1, 1848, Elkhorn, Wisc., reports that Lyman proposed the bill "authorizing an index to be made by myself" (*cit.* Gunn, *op. cit.,* p. 254); the State Historical Society of Wisconsin holds the ms. of this bill, which passed the Council Mar. 1848, but was rejected by the House Mar. 7, 1848. Therefore, the Letter of Oliver Cowdery to Brigham Young, Feb. 27, 1848, Elkhorn, Wisc. (LDS Historian's Office), must refer to this contemplated responsibility of indexing the territorial laws.

comment about possible "great political events" and the long
discussion of his determination to reunite with the Latter-day
Saints and migrate to Utah. One must conclude that his campaign, then in progress, was not what he had his heart set
upon at that time.[43]

The unsuccessful election attempt merely postponed
Oliver Cowdery's reconciliation with the Mormon Church
and people, which took place at Kanesville during October,
1848. In the meantime he co-edited for a short time the
ailing *Walworth County Democrat*. He is congratulated at
the beginning of July on his new position with the compli-
ment, "Mr. Cowdery is highly spoken of as an editor."[44] At his
return to the Latter-day Saints at "the Bluffs,"[45] Cowdery's
newspaper experience was utilized on a mechanical level as
Orson Hyde wrote on November 10, 1848, "Brother Oliver
Cowdery has assisted me to put up my press today."[46]

One can only speculate upon the reaction of the former
Democratic campaigner and editor to find that the Mormons
at Kanesville were voting as a block for the Whig party and
that his services were in demand for the publication of the
Frontier Guardian, which was intended to support the Whig
cause.[47] While this incongruous situation may in part explain

[43]Letter of Oliver Cowdery to Phineas Young, April 16, 1848, Elkhorn
Wisc., *cit.* Gunn, *op. cit.*, pp. 255-57. For the account of the relatively recent
discovery of this letter and others similarly cited from Gunn, see speech of
President Alonzo A. Hinckley, LDS General Conference Reports, April, 1934,
pp. 126-29.

[44]*Racine Advocate*, July 26, 1848. The single issue surviving from Cowdery's editorship (Aug. 4, 1848) lists his name on the masthead.

[45]The six extant Cowdery letters from 1848 and 1849 are filled with
references to "the Bluffs" (this shortened form of Council Bluffs appears eight
times) or the synonymous Kanesville. Although Cowdery's return to the LDS
Church has been challenged on insufficient grounds, his own letters (and much
additional evidence) settle this question by recording his plans before the
event and a retrospective reference afterward: "Now, my intention is, as soon
as I can get through with my liabilities here, to come up to the Bluffs. Iowa,
you know is my place of residence since the time we crossed the Mississippi
last fall." Letter of Oliver Cowdery to Phineas Young, June 24, 1849, Richmond,
Mo., *cit.* Gunn. *op. cit.*, p. 259.

[46]Letter of Orson Hyde to Wilford Woodruff, Nov. 10, 1848, Kanesville
(LDS Historian's Office).

[47]Although later rebuked by Brigham Young for imposing politics upon
religious leadership, Orson Hyde, the regional Church leader, had publicly
requested the Mormons to vote the Whig ticket just before Cowdery's return,

the rather short stay of Cowdery at Council Bluffs, in the absence of any direct evidence, the historian is only safe to assign economic reality as the basic reason why the Cowderys left Kanesville that winter. A cursory contact with Mormon journals shows that scores of others had to do the same thing; the Mormon "city" was really an outfitting point and not at all a center of population, business, or manufacturing. Since most of Elizabeth Whitmer Cowdery's relatives were some 200 miles southeast at Richmond, Missouri, that is where Cowdery temporarily located. With neither funds nor health to complete his intended migration west the following summer, he remained in Missouri while his chronic lung condition worsened to impose death, March 3, 1850. Three letters from this last year of his life in Richmond disclose the sincerity of his religious reconciliation, but fail to disclose professional activity, perhaps a symptom of his failing strength. There are no known law cases from this final location, and perhaps there was little or no legal practise, since Cowdery was economically secure in the care of close relatives. There is even reason to think that he planned to set aside his profession of law in returning to Mormon society.

One of the members of the Ray County bar in the last year of Cowdery's life was Alexander Doniphan, who in several later interviews remembered Oliver Cowdery favorably. With at least the agreement, if not the initiative, of this former acquaintance, the Circuit Court and bar declared a period of mourning for "our deceased friend," adjourned for the funeral, and passed a resolution of condolence to the widow, together with an expression of regret that, "in the death of our friend and brother, Oliver Cowdery, his profession has lost an accomplished member, and the community a valuable and worthy citizen."[48] The report of

---

an action which resulted in a solid Whig vote in the Mormon area but also the public scorn of the important Democratic newspapers of the state. For a summary, see J. Keith Melville, *Highlights in Mormon Political History*, Charles E. Merrill Monograph Series, No. 2 (May, 1967), pp. 1-37.

[48]Circuit Court Record, Ray County, Missouri, Book C, p. 190 (Mar. 5, 1850).

death did not reach his former home of Tiffin, Ohio, until
late that year. With slight inaccuracy of detail, but with
deep feeling about this former associate, John Breslin ran the
following story in the *Seneca Advertiser:*

> We are pained to learn, as we do by a letter from Independence, of
> the death of our much esteemed friend and former fellow citizen, OLIVER
> COWDERY. He died in Missouri, sometime during last summer, though
> at what place our correspondent does not inform us. His disease was con-
> sumption. His numerous acquaintances at this place will receive the tidings
> of his decease with much regret. He was a man of more than ordinary
> ability, and during his residence among us had endeared himself to all
> who knew him in the private and social walks of life.[49]

[49]*Seneca Advertiser*, Nov. 1, 1850.

The Book of Mormon:
A Blessing or
A Curse?

Monte S. Nyman

MONTE S. NYMAN is best known in seminaries and institutes of the Church where his course of study for teaching the Book of Mormon has been used for many years. He is assistant professor of ancient scripture and area coordinator of the Old and New Testament classes at Brigham Young University.

He has written numerous lessons for the Sunday School Gospel Doctrine manuals and is a frequent contributor to the Church magazines. Dr. Nyman is currently bishop of the Edgemont 2nd Ward, Edgemont Stake.

He holds bachelor's and master's degrees from Utah State University and completed his doctoral studies at BYU. He was a high school coach before joining the seminary and institute program.

He is married to the former Mary Ann Sullivan and they have eight children.

THE BOOK OF MORMON:
A BLESSING OR A CURSE?

Monte S. Nyman

The seven-by-five-inch, one-inch thick book of 521 pages that we call the Book of Mormon is evidence of a movement on earth that is a fulfillment of a prophecy spoken by Moses and reiterated by the Apostle Peter:

> For Moses truly said unto the fathers, A prophet shall the Lord your God raise up unto you of your brethren, like unto me; him shall ye hear in all things whatsoever he shall say unto you.

> And it shall come to pass, that every soul, which will not hear that prophet, shall be destroyed from among the people. (Acts 3:22-23.)

On the night of September 21 and the morning of September 22, 1823, a young man by the name of Joseph Smith was visited by an angel who introduced himself as "a messenger sent from the presence of God, and that his name was Moroni; that God had a work for me [Joseph Smith] to do." (Joseph Smith 2:33.)

After informing him of "a book deposited, written upon gold plates, giving an account of the former inhabitants of this continent, and the source from whence they sprang," he quoted several biblical prophecies including "the third chapter of Acts, twenty-second and twenty-third verses, precisely as they stand in our New Testament. He said that that prophet was Christ; but the day had not yet come when 'they who would not hear his voice should be cut off from among the people,' but soon would come." (Joseph Smith 2:36-40.)

Joseph Smith has instructed us that the Savior often referred to this later work in his parables.

. . . The kingdom of heaven is like to a grain of mustard seed, which a man took, and sowed in his field:

Which indeed is the least of all seeds: but when it is grown, it is the greatest among herbs, and becometh a tree, so that the birds of the air come and lodge in the branches thereof. (Matthew 13:31-32.)

Joseph Smith gave the following interpretation of the above parable.

. . . we can discover plainly that this figure is given to represent the Church as it shall come forth in the last days. Behold, the Kingdom of Heaven is likened unto it. Now, what is like unto it?

Let us take the Book of Mormon, which a man took and hid in his field, securing it by his faith, to spring up in the last days, or in due time; let us behold it coming forth out of the ground, which is indeed accounted the least of all seeds, but behold it branching forth, yea, even towering, with lofty branches, and God-like majesty, until it, like the mustard seed, becomes the greatest of all herbs. And it is truth, and it has sprouted and come forth out of the earth, and righteousness begins to look down from heaven, and God is sending down His powers, gifts, and angels, to lodge in the branches thereof. (*Teachings of the Prophet Joseph Smith*, page 98.)

The influence that the Book of Mormon would have on the world was further demonstrated by one of the Savior's parables of the kingdom.

Another parable spake he unto them: The kingdom of heaven is like unto leaven, which a woman took, and hid in three measures of meal, till the whole was leavened. (Matthew 13:33.)

Joseph Smith's explanation of this parable shows its relationship to the world.

. . . It may be understood that the Church of the Latter-day Saints has taken its rise from a little leaven that was put into three witnesses. Behold, how much this is like the parable! It is fast leavening the lump, and will soon leaven the whole. . . . (*Teachings of the Prophet Joseph Smith*, page 100.)

This latter-day movement's association to the former-day movement was likewise given by the Savior through parable.

Then said he (Jesus) unto them, Therefore every scribe which is instructed unto the kingdom of heaven is like unto a man that is an householder, which bringeth forth out of his treasure things new and old. (Matthew 13:52.)

The latter-day prophet Joseph Smith gave this explanation of the parable.

For the works of this example, see the Book of Mormon coming forth out of the treasure of the heart. Also the covenants given to the Latter-day Saints, also the translation of the Bible—thus bringing forth out of the heart things new and old, thus answering to three measures of meal undergoing the purifying touch by a revelation of Jesus Christ, and the ministering of angels, who have already commenced this work in the last days, which will answer to the leaven which leavened the whole lomp. Amen. (*Teachings of the Prophet Joseph Smith*, page 102.)

When The Church of Jesus Christ of Latter-day Saints was restored, the Lord gave a revelation concerning the contents and purposes of the Book of Mormon and then made this significant declaration:

Therefore, having so great witnesses, by them shall the world be judged, even as many as shall hereafter come to a knowledge of this work. (D&C 20:13.)

Thus the Book of Mormon is restored in these latter days to bring judgment to all who possess this unique volume of scripture. A careful study of the book itself and other related revelations and teachings discloses that this judgment will take place in three steps or phases which may overlap but yet are separate in nature.

The first phase will be the gathering of the seed of Ephraim from the nations of the Gentiles where they were scattered during the various times of the dispersion of Israel. The second phase will be the cleansing of those gathered or the cutting off from the Lord's people those who will not hearken unto his voice. The final phase will be the judgments of God coming upon the nations who have had the seed of Ephraim gathered out and the remaining people, having rejected the Book of Mormon, will experience the natural calamities that will follow the withdrawing of the Spirit of the Lord from them because of their wickedness. The entire future of the world has been shown to many prophets throughout history including several Book of Mormon prophets. Their teachings form the basis for the three judgments identified above and verify the significance of the Book of Mormon in each phase.

Phase I of this division, the gathering out of the seed of Joseph, primarily Ephraim, from among the nations of the earth is attested to by Nephi. After bearing testimony that Jesus Christ is the only name under heaven whereby man can be saved, he states that the Book of Mormon will be instrumental in gathering Joseph's seed:

> Wherefore, for this cause the Lord God promised unto me that these things which I write shall be kept and preserved, and handed down unto my seed from generation to generation, that the promise may be fulfilled unto Joseph, that his seed should never perish as long as the earth should stand. (2 Nephi 25:21.)

Joseph of Egypt was also promised by the Lord that a righteous branch of his seed would be remembered by the covenants of the Lord in the latter days, and that the Messiah should be made manifest unto them. (See 2 Nephi 3:5.)

The prophet Mormon, father of Moroni, the angelic visitor to Joseph Smith, likewise prophesied that Joseph's seed was to gather as part of this great movement.

> Yea, and surely shall he again bring a remnant of the seed of Joseph to the knowledge of the Lord their God.
> And as surely as the Lord liveth, will he gather in from the four quarters of the earth all the remnant of the seed of Jacob, who are scattered abroad upon all the face of the earth. (3 Nephi 5:23-24.)

Joseph's seed will be gathered because they will recognize the words of Christ contained within the Book of Mormon, as Jesus said:

. . . I told you, and ye believed not: the works that I do in my Father's name, they bear witness of me.

But ye believe not, because ye are not of my sheep, as I said unto you.

My sheep hear my voice, and I know them, and they follow me: (John 10:25-27.)

As the Book of Mormon goes forth to the nations of the earth, the voice of Christ or the good shepherd calls unto them and those of the seed of Joseph recognize this familiar voice. Those who hearken become the followers of Christ while those who do not become the followers of the devil and thus the division is formed.

Alma also plainly taught this concept:

Behold, I say unto you, that the good shepherd doth call you; yea, and in his own name he doth call you, which is the name of Christ; and if ye will not hearken unto the voice of the good shepherd, to the name by which ye are called, behold, ye are not the sheep of the good shepherd.

And now if ye are not the sheep of the good shepherd, of what fold are ye? Behold, I say unto you, that the devil is your shepherd, and ye are of his fold; and now, who can deny this? Behold, I say unto you, whosoever denieth this is a liar and a child of the devil. (Alma 5:38-39.)

Many Church members who have come from among the Gentiles have had their lineage affirmed by revelation (patriarchal blessings) and are primarily of the seed of Ephraim, and thus are of Joseph. That this is literal and not adoptive is confirmed in D&C 86:8-9 where priesthood holders are told that they are the literal seed according to the flesh and have been hid from the world with Christ in God.

Phase II of the latter-day movement, the cutting off of those who will not hearken to the Lord's voice, was also clearly taught by the Savior in his parables of the kingdom.

Again, the kingdom of heaven is like unto a net, that was cast into the sea, and gathered of every kind:

Which, when it was full, they drew to shore, and sat down, and gathered the good into vessels, but cast the bad away. (Matthew 13:47-48.)

Joseph Smith explained how this applied to the seed of Joseph.

> . . . behold, the seed of Joseph, spreading forth the Gospel net upon the face of the earth, gathering of every kind, that the good may be saved in vessels prepared for that purpose and the angels will take care of the bad. So shall it be at the end of the world—the angels shall come forth and sever the wicked from among the just, and cast them into the furnace of fire, and there shall be wailing and gnashing of teeth. (*Teachings of the Prophet Joseph Smith*, p. 102.)

Nephi likewise testified of a time when there would be a great division among the people.

> For the time speedily cometh that the Lord God shall cause a great division among the people, and the wicked will be destroyed; and he will spare his people, yea, even if it so be that he must destroy the wicked by fire. (2 Nephi 30:10.)

It should be noted that the Lord God will cause this great division and that it will be consummated with the destruction of the wicked. While this destruction carries tones of the ushering in of the millennium, the time period will undoubtedly be an extended one. The Lord has designated that the beginning of this destruction will be among the seed of Joseph, or His people:

> Behold, vengeance cometh speedily upon the inhabitants of the earth, a day of wrath, a day of burning, a day of desolation, of weeping, of mourning, and of lamentation; and as a whirlwind it shall come upon all the face of the earth, saith the Lord.
>
> And upon my house shall it begin, and from my house shall it go forth, saith the Lord.
>
> First among those among you, saith the Lord, who have professed to know my name and have not known me, and have blasphemed against me in the midst of my house, saith the Lord. (D&C 112:24-26.)

Through studying the Book of Mormon and hearkening to the voice of Christ within it, we can associate ourselves with the Lord's people and come to know him, but if we do not study it or hearken to it, we do not come to know him and we cut ourselves off from among his people. A few examples will suffice. Studying the Book of Mormon will show us that knowledge must continually grow through revelation (see 2 Nephi 28:26-30); that we must beware of the philosophies of men that will be prevalent (see 2 Nephi 28:4-8); that studying the scriptures leads one to eternal life (see 1 Nephi 15:24-25; Alma 37:44-46; Helaman 3:29-30); that plain and precious parts have been lost from the Bible causing the Gentiles to stumble (see 1 Nephi 13:23-24; 14:1; 2 Nephi 26:20-21); that the priesthood is very significant in our lives (see Alma 13 and Jacob 1:17-19); that priest-craft is forbidden (see 2 Nephi 26:28-31); and that those who follow the Book of Mormon teachings will be united into a Zion people through the gift and power of the Holy Ghost (see 1 Nephi 13:37 and Moses 7:18.)

The first two phases of this latter-day movement will be on an individual and personal basis. Every man who has an opportunity to read a copy of the Book of Mormon will be held accountable not only for accepting it but also for living its teachings. This is verified by the Lord when he enumerates the various records or books which he commands to be written:

. . . for out of the books which shall be written, I will judge the world, every man according to their works, according to that which is written. (2 Nephi 29:11.)

The judgment will begin with each individual as he chooses to accept or reject the Book of Mormon and its teachings, but it will not be completed until each individual stands face to face with the authors of the Book of Mormon. All four of the major writers of the Book of Mormon have testified concerning their part in this judgment. Nephi concluded his part of the record by saying:

And if they are not the words of Christ, judge ye—for Christ will show unto you, with power and great glory, that they are his words, at the last day; and you and I shall stand face to face before his bar; and ye shall know that I have been commanded of him to write these things, notwithstanding my weakness. (2 Nephi 33:11-15.)

Jacob bears similar testimony:

Finally, I bid you farewell, until I shall meet you before the pleasing bar of God, which bar striketh the wicked with awful dread and fear. Amen. (Jacob 6:13.)

Mormon, although he does not bear it in quite the same way as the other writers, gave quite a discourse about his position as a special witness of the Lord Jesus Christ. He utterly refused to go up against their enemies any more but stood as an idle witness unto the world as he had been commanded of the Lord to do. He addresses himself unto the various groups, the Gentiles and the house of Israel (see Mormon 3:16-22).

Moroni bears this convincing testimony as he concludes the entire record.

And I exhort you to remember these things; for the time speedily cometh that ye shall know that I lie not, for you shall see me at the bar of God; and the Lord God will say unto you: Did I not declare my words unto you; which were written by this man, like as one crying from the dead, yea, even as one speaking out of the dust?

I declare these things unto the fulfilling of the prophecies. And behold, they shall proceed forth out of the mouth of the everlasting God; and his word shall hiss forth from generation to generation.

And God shall show unto you that that which I have written is true. (Moroni 10:27-29.)

Judging, in our modern terminology, could be translated "witnessing." Just as Moroni, Nephi, and Jacob are going to be at that judgment bar, so will the apostles chosen by Christ, and they will witness that Jesus is the Christ. The twelve in Jerusalem will witness that he was born among them, came to them and called them as his special witnesses, that they viewed his great ministry wherein he performed great miracles, viewed his atonement as far as they were able to do so, and his crucifixion and resurrection. The twelve apostles of this continent, the Nephite disciples as they are known, will bear testimony that they witnessed the Savior coming to this continent and teaching the gospel as it is found within the Book of Mormon. The apostles of this dispensation will undoubtedly also be at that judgment bar to witness to each one that they bore testimony of Christ and his teachings of salvation.

Phase III shows the Book of Mormon judging the world on a nation basis.

> Wherefore, these things shall go from generation to generation as long as the earth shall stand; and they shall go according to the will and pleasure of God; and the nations who shall possess them shall be judged of them, according to the words which are written. (2 Nephi 25:21.)

How can a nation be judged by the Book of Mormon? It will be in a very natural way. The land of America belongs to the seed of Joseph. A New Jerusalem, a Holy City unto the Lord, will be built upon this land and it will become the land of Joseph (see Ether 13:8; 3 Nephi 20:22). Jerusalem will also be built up again, a holy city unto the Lord and the Book of Mormon will be instrumental in restoring the Jews to their inheritance. As the seed of Joseph are gathered to Zion and the seed of Judah are gathered to Jerusalem the rest of the nations of the world will be subjected to the judgments of God.

> Now these things are written unto the remnant of the house of Jacob; and they are written after this manner, because it is known of God that wickedness will not bring them forth unto them; and they are to be hid up unto the Lord that they may come forth in his own due time. And behold, they shall go unto the unbelieving of the Jews; and for this intent shall they go—that they may be persuaded that Jesus is the Christ, the Son of the living God; that the Father may bring about, through his most Beloved, his great and eternal purpose, in restoring the Jews, or all the house of Israel, to the land of their inheritance, which the Lord their God hath given them, unto the fulfilling of his covenant; (Mormon 5:12, 14; also Ether 13:5.)

It will be what the scriptures call the fulness of the times of the Gentiles, when the men of God and the scriptures will be taken from among them.

> And thus commandeth the Father that I should say unto you: At that day when the Gentiles shall sin against my gospel, and shall be lifted up in the pride of their hearts above all nations, and above all the people of the whole earth, and shall be filled with all manner of lyings, and of deceits, and of mischiefs, and all manner of hypocrisy, and murders, and priestcrafts, and whoredoms, and of secret abominations; and if they shall do all those things, and shall reject the fulness of my gospel, saith the Father, I will bring the fulness of my gospel from among them. (3 Nephi 16:10.)

When that time comes and those sins and abominations are among the Gentiles, the spirit of the Lord will withdraw and leave them to their own destruction. The Book of Mormon testifies that this very thing happened among the Nephites (see 2 Nephi 26:11 and Mormon 5:16).

As the Lord has gathered his people into selected regions, he will prevent them from being destroyed. Nephi commenting on Isaiah makes reference to this particular time.

> Wherefore he [the Lord] will preserve the righteous by his power, even if it so be that the fulness of his wrath must come, and the righteous be preserved, even unto the destruction of their enemies by fire. Wherefore, the righteous need not fear; for thus saith the prophet, they shall be saved, even if it so be as by fire. (1 Nephi 22:17.)

And also Isaiah says:

> And the Lord will create upon every dwelling-place of mount Zion and upon her assemblies, a cloud and smoke by day and shining of a flaming fire by night; For upon all the glory of Zion shall be a defense. (2 Nephi 14:5.)

The promise is that the Lord will protect those who have gathered unto their chosen places with the literal fire of glory hovering over them as it hovered over the children of Israel when they were in the wilderness. Nephi, earlier, saw this same thing when the saints of God were small but scattered among the whole face of the earth. They were protected by the power of God and the righteousness of the people (see 1 Nephi 14:14).

What will be the condition in those areas from which the Spirit has withdrawn? Nephi's comments upon Isaiah describe their condition:

> And the blood of that great and abominable church, which is the whore of all the earth, shall turn upon their own heads; for they shall war among themselves, and the sword of their own hands shall fall upon their own heads, and they shall be drunken with their own blood. (1 Nephi 22:13.)

This great internal conflict was also seen by the Prophet Joseph Smith in a vision:

> The time is soon coming, when no man will have any peace but in Zion and her stakes.
>
> I saw men hunting the lives of their own sons, and brother murdering brother, women killing their own daughters, and daughters seeking the lives of their mothers. I saw armies arrayed against armies. I saw blood, desolation, fires. The Son of Man has said that the mother shall be against the daughter, and the daughter against the mother. (*Teachings of the Prophet Joseph Smith,* page 161.)

While many nations will be in a state of civil war, Nephi says, that there will also be war among nations:

> And every nation which shall war against thee, O house of Israel, shall be turned one against another, and they shall fall into the pit which they digged to ensnare the people of the Lord. And all that fight against Zion shall be destroyed, and that great whore, who hath perverted the right ways of the Lord, yea, that great and abominable church, shall tumble to the dust and great shall be the fall of it. (1 Nephi 22:14.)

It will come to be as Mormon said, a case of the wicked destroying the wicked:

> But, behold, the judgments of God will overtake the wicked; and it is by the wicked that the wicked are punished; for it is the wicked that stir up the hearts of the children of men unto bloodshed. (Mormon 4:5.)

Thus the Lord will judge the world in righteousness (2 Nephi 30:9).

Other prophets, Enoch for example, were also shown that the Lord would raise up a righteous generation which would believe his truth as it came out of the earth:

> And the day shall come that the earth shall rest, but before that day the heavens shall be darkened, and a veil of darkness shall cover the earth; and the heavens shall shake, and also the earth; and great tribulations shall be among the children of men, but my people will I preserve;
>
> And righteousness will I send down out of heaven; and truth will I send forth out of the earth, to bear testimony of mine Only Begotten; his resurrection from the dead; yea, and also the resurrection of all men; and righteouness and truth will I cause to sweep the earth as with a flood; to gather out mine elect from the four quarters of the earth, unto a place which I shall prepare, an Holy City, that my people may gird up their loins, and be looking forth for the time of my coming; for there shall be my tabernacle, and it shall be called Zion, a New Jerusalem. (Moses 7:61-62.)

The Book of Mormon bears avid testimony that righteousness has come down from heaven and truth has risen from the earth to bear testimony of Jesus Christ, his resurrection, the gathering of Israel, and all the other facts identified by Enoch above.

We have today a Book of Mormon, 521 pages in length, that many of us have setting on our shelves and never open. Yet it is probably the most significant piece of literature that any of us could have in our homes. It will judge the world, it will be an instrument in saving the world, and it will be like a two-edged sword, which we cannot take hold of in any way without being cut by it. Remember that Laman and Lemuel argued with Nephi about some of the things that they could not understand and Nephi said to them: "it [the truth] cutteth them to the very center." (1 Nephi 16:2) The Book of Mormon will penetrate, it will bear testimony, and it will condemn. It will be a blessing or a curse for us.

INDEX

—H—

happiness, self-denial promotes, 33
He Smashed It Before My Eyes, 66
heaven, Joseph Smith on building kingdom of, 5
Hobbes, Thomas, on nature of man, 105
Holiness, Man of, 112
home, Brigham Young on earth as, 6
hunger, Dostoevsky on, 98
Hyde, John, case of, 171

—I—

illumined man, 121
implementing and understanding principles, 75
improvement, Brigham Young on, 8, 17
insanity, sin is, 94

—J—

Johnny Lingo, 82
Joseph, seed of, 224

—K—

Kant on morality, 48
killing animals, Brigham Young on, 18
killing in sport, Joseph F. Smith on, 22
Kimball, J. Golden, story of, 181
kingdom of heaven, Joseph Smith on building, 5
knowledge of self, obtaining, 74

—L—

laws, violation of spiritual, 93
Leibman, Joshua Loth, personal experience of, 110
Lewis, C. S., on essence of religion, 61; on relationship with God, 100
life, David O. McKay on purpose of, 145; light as, 129; meaning of, 44
life's meaning, 37; meaning and commitment, 33
light as beauty, 128; as good, 127; as life, 129; as real, 122; as truth, 123
limited loving, 66
line, sensitive, 80
literary skill, Prophet Joseph Smith's, 151
living church, 97
love, B. West Belnap on capacity to, 58; Church is organized, 90; divine

definition of, 72; meaning of, 65; unconditional, 98; limited, 66
loyal behavior, 186
loyalty, reciprocity law of, 190

—M—

man illumined, 121
man, John Donne on importance of each, 79; Mormonism and nature of, 137; Nietzsche on, 44; Thomas Hobbes on nature of, 105
Man of Holiness, 112
Marcel, Gabriel, on fidelity, 47
maturity, emotional, 77; in personality, 76; physical, 77; social, 77; spiritual, 78
McKay, David O., on purpose of life, 145
meaning, guidelines to divine, 65; of life, 44
meaninglessness of natural life, 39
medicine, gospel has preventive, 93; gospel has redemptive, 94
Messiah, mission of, 112
mission of Messiah, 112
model, Savior as our, 73
moral cleanliness, Brigham Young on, 4
morality, Kant on, 48
Mormonism and nature of man, 137

—N—

natural life, meaninglessness of, 39
natural man doctrine, 37
nature of man, Mormonism and, 137; Thomas Hobbes on, 105
network of relationships, 79
New Jerusalem, 227
Nietzsche on man, 44

—O—

obedience, Boyd K. Packer on, 51
obedience is pleading of Father, 90
object of commitment, 45
obtaining knowledge of self, 74
organized love, Church is, 90
orthodoxy, thrill of, 99

—P—

Packer, Boyd K., on obedience, 51
participation, sign of loyalty, 188
peace, 105; of God, 117; permanent world, 116
Peace, Prince of, 112
Peirce, C. S., on self-control, 50

—Y—

yesterday, inherit, 90
Young, Brigham on Babylon, 26; on
  conservation, 10; on crickets, 23;
  on cultivating taste, 9; on earth as
  home, 6; on environment, 3; on fire
  safety, 18; on improvement, 8, 17;
  on killing animals, 18; on loving
  earth, 13; on moral cleanliness, 4;
  on physical cleanliness, 4; on pollution, 4; on priesthood as power
  over all, 29; on property of earth,
  17; on reverence for everything, 19;
  on right of property, 14; on Satan's
  labor to destroy earth, 28; on waste,
  12, 16
Young, Brigham Bicknell, 173
youth of Zion, 89

—Z—

Zion, youth of, 89